Program Design and Implementation

PAID Time Off
BANKS

M. Michael Markowich, D.P.A.
Author of *Paying & Managing Absences*

About WorldatWork®

WorldatWork (www.worldatwork.org) is the association for human resources professionals focused on attracting, motivating and retaining employees. Founded in 1955, WorldatWork provides practitioners with knowledge leadership to effectively implement total rewards— compensation, benefits, work-life, performance and recognition, development and career opportunities—by connecting employee engagement to business performance. WorldatWork supports its 30,000 members and customers in 30 countries with thought leadership, education, publications, research and certification.

The WorldatWork group of registered marks includes: WorldatWork®, workspan®, Certified Compensation Professional or CCP®, Certified Benefits Professional® or CBP, Global Remuneration Professional or GRP®, Work-Life Certified Professional or WLCP™, WorldatWork Society of Certified Professionals®, and Alliance for Work-Life Progress® or AWLP®.

WorldatWork Staff Contributors

Dan Cafaro

Rebecca Williams Ficker

Christina Fuoco

Alan Luu

Wendy Anderson

Lenny Sanicola, CCP, CBP, GRP, CEBS, SPHR

WorldatWork.
The Total Rewards Association
www.worldatwork.org

Dedication

This guidebook is dedicated to my wife Nancy and my three children, Shari, Jonathan and Paul.

Table of Contents

Introduction

WorldatWork prepared this guidebook about paid time off (PTO) banks to help you increase productivity and lower costs by reducing unscheduled absences. The material is presented in a conversational tone so you can learn how to assess, cost-justify, design, communicate and implement a cost-effective PTO program for your company.

This comprehensive, updated version of the popular 2000 edition contains new information, strategies and tactics, including:

- Expanded communication strategies to overcome resistance to change and to obtain managerial and employee buy-in. These include:
  - PTO policy and procedure statements used by various companies to explain PTO to workers.
  - Employee handouts explaining PTO to employees. Examples are provided to show how companies communicate key PTO plan components to employees.
  - Script used to "break the ice" when presenting PTO to employee groups. Breaking the ice is often stressful, and the first few minutes of your presentation are critical for setting the right tone. The script will give you a real-world idea of how to effectively begin your explanation to employees.
  - Answers to some of the most common questions about PTO. This is an excellent overview and highlights the many steps of PTO planning.
  - Description of how change theories give guidance for PTO implementation. Conversion to PTO is really the end result of a "change process." However, most people are suspicious of change, even though we live in an era of change. You will find the classic change theories helpful because they give direction about how to overcome resistance to change and how to obtain employee support for PTO.
  - Lessons learned about how *not* to implement new benefit programs. There are two basic ways to learn. One way is from your own experience, and the other is from the experience and mistakes of others. The latter is often preferred because it is less painful and costly to you. You might be

surprised by the decisions top managers made in the example that is presented. However, that example alerts you to "potholes" to avoid as you plan to implement PTO.

- Answers to 58 questions asked by managers during a WorldatWork live Web chat about PTO. This Q&A Web chat provides an informal explanation of a broad range of PTO-related issues. You will find the material easy to read and the answers brief and to the point.

• Expanded formulas for you to use when conducting the fiscal analysis. A special feature of this guidebook is the presentation and explanation of formulas for you to use to cost-justify PTO design features. HR professionals have asked us for assistance with this number-crunching activity, and so to further assist you, you will find that numbers are included in the formulas to give you a "real company" example of applying them. All you will need to do is plug in your company's numbers in the formulas to quantify and analyze your absentee situation. You will find a worksheet included to assist you. The results of using these formulas will drive your PTO planning efforts and help you convince top management of the fiscal integrity of your PTO plan.

• Linkage of PTO with the WorldatWork Total Rewards Model. PTO exemplifies the positive features highlighted in the WorldatWork Total Reward Model— another reason why PTO's use and popularity are growing.

• A new and updated case study to help you learn from the 13-year PTO experience of Rockford Memorial Hospital (Ill.). The company and workers enjoy positive results. Much can be learned from Rockford's experience, especially how it addressed major employee concerns at the time of conversion to PTO, and how over time PTO has dramatically increased attendance (and as a side benefit has increased productivity and morale) and produced a significant decrease in costs associated with unscheduled absences.

• Updated WorldatWork survey on PTO use and effectiveness. It is always helpful to know how other companies view PTO. These survey results reinforce PTO's value and growth in all industries as reported.

How to View PTO

PTO involves a different way of thinking about paid time off. Many employees see paid time off as a "use or lose" benefit. However, PTO actually changes the ground rules. With PTO, workers have a bank of time to use. It is their time—not their company's time. Therefore, abusing their own time is less appealing.

PTO helps companies control costs and gives employees greater flexibility to meet their personal and family obligations. An important and valuable by-product of PTO is a significant improvement in the communication between managers and employees. Managers find out in advance when time off is needed by workers (instead of when workers call in sick), and in return managers become more amenable to grant specific requests for paid time off (even in increments of 15 minutes, in addition to hours or days).

Scheduled absences are less of a problem than unexpected absences that catch managers off guard. PTO motivates employees to think first about scheduling time off in advance rather than using unscheduled absences for the time they need when nonwork issues arise. Companies prefer PTO because of this major benefit. Employees also benefit because managers are more flexible in their response to requests for time off. It is really a win–win outcome for everyone.

Skills Required for Development and Implementation of PTO

Development and implementation of a PTO plan require many skills, including:

- **Conceptual skills:** Understanding how various PTO components come together. This guidebook identifies the key features.
- **Analytical skills:** Conducting fiscal analysis to support cost-effective design. HR professionals should involve fiscal officers in this important activity. There is considerable power in letting the numbers speak for themselves.
- **Persuasive skills:** Obtaining buy-in from constituents and overcoming resistance. This guidebook provides explanations for many of the strategies and techniques used successfully by companies that implement PTO.
- **Communication skills:** Developing clear and concise written material and being comfortable in the role of messenger. Examples of PTO policy and procedure statements and handouts in the guidebook give you ideas for developing your own literature.
- **Strategic skills:** Linking business objectives to company support for conversion to PTO. You can apply the WorldatWork Total Reward Model to show PTO's value and how it contributes to your company's ability to meet its corporate business objectives.
- **Organizational skills:** PTO requires the efforts of a team of people. Therefore, it is essential to build an internal network of support among all affected employees and to adhere to a projected time schedule. Many of your company's managers and employees should be asked to contribute to PTO's success. This guidebook describes who these people are and how they can help you in the design and in the implementation of your PTO plan. The HR

professional's role is like that of an orchestra's conductor. It is important to keep the process going and make sure all components required for a successful PTO plan are handled correctly. Again, this guidebook identifies all key components.

When and Why PTO Started

PTO started in the health-care industry in the early 1970s. Because hospitals operate around the clock seven days a week, their female workers (about 75 percent of hospital employees are female) were having problems meeting work and nonwork needs. Many female workers also had home responsibilities that added extra strain. In response to this problem, hospitals looked to PTO as an answer.

In the mid-1980s, the author of this guidebook conducted a national research study of methods to control unscheduled absences in hospitals. The study found PTO was the most effective way hospitals could reduce such absences. Subsequent studies conducted by the author and others have confirmed that finding—in the health-care industry and in all other industries as well.

PTO's Impact

During each year of a 16-year span (1991 to 2006), Commerce Clearing House's (CCH) *Unscheduled Absence Survey* compared PTO to other prominent absentee control programs and concluded PTO was the most effective program.

PTO has increased in popularity in all industries, including health care; the percentage of respondents to the CCH *Unscheduled Absence Survey* who use PTO plans has steadily grown. In 2006, 70 percent of respondents reported using PTO plans, while only 16 percent used them in 1991.

According to a 2006 *WorldatWork Hot Topic Survey*, 64 percent of the 679 surveyed companies reported having a PTO bank system for their employees (33 percent) or indicated they are considering implementing one (31 percent). Other national surveys report similar usage and effectiveness.

What is clear from these results is unscheduled absences, if not controlled, will result in a competitive disadvantage for companies. Based on survey results, Corporate America acknowledges unscheduled absences are costly and PTO is a viable antidote.

Getting Ready for PTO 1

Design and implementation of a PTO plan require the involvement of many company officials. A successful PTO plan is the result of an effective team effort. An HR executive or a director of benefits can be the group leader. A diversity of opinion and the relevant expertise of PTO task force members greatly enhance the quality of PTO design and facilitate PTO's acceptance by top executives.

The following steps are recommended:

1. **Make a complete assessment.** (See Chapter 2.)

2. **Consider business pressures that support need to control unscheduled absences.** Meeting business pressures are important for your company's success and serve as reasons for PTO when talking with other managers and employees. Examples include:

    a. New competition to your company's products or services

    b. Necessity of controlling benefit costs to maintain a competitively priced product or service.

3. **Identify members of PTO managerial task force.** These include:

    a. *Chief Financial Officer (CFO) or designee:* Fiscal expertise is needed to help with the fiscal analysis phase. Also, you will want the CFO to validate the accuracy of the PTO program's fiscal impact to the Chief Executive Officer (CEO). Having the company's "numbers person" support your position carries a lot of weight with top executives.

    b. *Other line executives:* Their input is important to ensure PTO meets employees' needs. Also, line executives can help sell PTO to top management.

    c. *Director of management information systems* or a designee can expedite processing of necessary reports for fiscal analysis.

    d. *Director of public relations or communications:* Having a sound communication strategy is extremely important. The public relations/communications representative can provide valuable guidance for verbal and written communications.

    e. *Director of benefits* (if that person is not the group leader)

    f. *HR executive* (if that person is not the group leader).

4. **Determine if you need a consultant and how a consultant can complement your expertise and your company's resources.**

5. **Gain executive support to proceed with PTO planning and ultimately obtain approval for implementation.** Top executives do not want to be surprised. Therefore, it is a good idea to keep top executives aware of the status of PTO planning throughout the process. The HR executive can provide the link to top management.

6. **Expect the full process of PTO planning and implementation to take between six months and 12 months.** It is better to have extra time built in so that you can fix any problems that may arise without having to rush to meet a closer deadline.

7. **Expect to invest considerable time, effort and energy.**

8. **Expect resistance to the PTO plan.** Whenever you implement a significant change, such as a conversion to PTO, some employees will have difficulty accepting it. The key to overcome this difficulty is how you manage the resistance. The section in this guidebook about communication and implementation strategies highlights ways to overcome resistance and achieve employee buy-in.

Assessment   2

n your assessment, the first question you should answer is, "Do you have an absentee problem?" If you do, you then need to determine its severity. The severity of the problem often reflects a company's inability to absorb the fiscal impact of employee absences, especially unscheduled ones. The second key question to answer is what the impact of future absentee costs will be. In essence, you need to determine the impact on the company to not make any changes to its current time-off practices.

The decision to change a company's absentee control approach usually means the company cannot afford current and projected absentee costs. Therefore, we suggest you complete a thorough assessment of your absentee situation.

You may need to contact other departments (e.g., fiscal, management information systems) for assistance. Afterward, you should review your conclusions with your supervisor to obtain reaction and support. Ultimately, the answers can serve as a basis for a proposal to top management that outlines the justification for changing your company's absentee management program.

As you answer the following questions during your assessment, think about what happens when employees are unable to report to work when scheduled. In other words:

1. Who does the work when scheduled workers are not present?
2. What are the costs when employees are absent?
3. Who takes care of your customers when scheduled workers are absent?
4. How do employees feel when they have to work harder to cover for absent workers?
5. How much managerial time is used to find replacements for absent workers (time that could be better used to address business issues)?
6. Where will your customers shop if they cannot receive appropriate service due to unscheduled absences? Have you lost customers because of the dissatisfaction?
7. Do employees with good attendance records become demoralized because certain employees take advantage of your sick-leave policies?

8. Are your employees using sick days to get additional time off with pay (whether they are sick or not)?

9. Do you have sufficient coverage to maintain productivity and profitability goals when employees call in sick?

10. Are unscheduled absences increasing? If yes, by what percentage?

11. Are employees having difficulty getting scheduled time off?

12. Do workers need greater flexibility to schedule time off to handle personal and family obligations?

13. What are the projected absentee costs for the next three years if the company decides not to make any changes in paid time off practices? In business, everything is relative. So it is important to assess your company's ability to absorb projected costs. This information will give top management another factor to consider when deciding whether or not changes in paid time off practices would be in the company's best interest.

PTO and the WorldatWork Total Rewards Model 3

n 2006, WorldatWork introduced a new total rewards model. (See Figure 3-1.) This model explains the interplay between employees' contribution of time, talent and efforts and the achievement of desired business objectives. A critical component of the model is what WorldatWork calls the "exchange relationship" between employer and employees. Employees receive tangible and intangible rewards that enrich their lives in exchange for helping the company meet its productivity goals.

Figure 3-1
WorldatWork Total Rewards Model

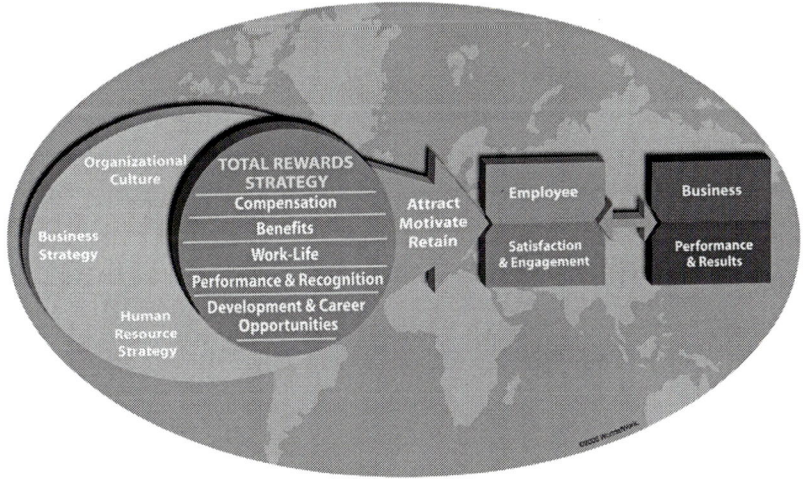

There has always been an exchange relationship between companies and employees. However, unprecedented challenges face companies today, and increased pressure to attract, motivate and retain workers exists. Contributing to this greater pressure are:

- Dramatic changes in the workplace, including increased awareness of conflicts caused by trying to balance family, home and work demands

- Workforce demographic changes that challenged the traditional model of earlier decades—a working father and a stay-at-home mother.

While program efficiencies and cost controls have been pivotal for company survival, many systems have recognized that an integrated and enriched "value exchange" between an employer and its employees can accelerate velocity and success.

How PTO Links with the WorldatWork Total Rewards Model

- **Lowers costs** by reducing unscheduled absences and thereby lowers replacement costs.
- **Enhances morale and retention** by helping employees address work–life needs.
- **Increases productivity** by increasing "presenteeism." Increase in attendance also has a positive impact on employee morale.
- **Improves customer satisfaction** by having more workers present to respond to customer demands. Just think how you would feel if you had to wait a very long time for service and then found out it was due to the salespeople or restaurant waitresses calling in sick. Or consider how you would feel waiting in line at your neighborhood bank, seeing empty teller booths and then finding out that the other tellers could not report to work as scheduled. It is a different feeling when you are the customer and not the employee.
- **Positively impacts corporate culture** by making scheduling time off flexible enough to balance employee needs with fulfilling business requirements.
- **Introduces new ways of thinking about traditional business practices**. Supports movement from a "command-and-control" managerial style and an employee entitlement mentality to a style that includes greater employee ownership and accountability as well as improved working relationships between managers and staff.
- **Becomes business and HR strategy.** PTO enhances a company's competitiveness and assists in the achievement of business objectives.

PTO Facts and Issues 4

Sick leave was originally designed as insurance to provide salary continuation for brief absences due to personal illnesses. Research shows employees call in sick (even when not ill) to get a day off to handle a personal or family obligation. The use of sick time sometimes occurs when an employee's manager turns down a request for time off. In many cases, a manager may feel work requires the employee's attendance. However, in other cases, employees only need one or two hours off—either before the shift or at the end, rather than a whole day. If the employee's requested time off is not granted, research has shown there is a high probability that the worker will call in sick. Consequently, the manager ends up spending time to find a replacement or actually doing the work. The worst scenario is the employee's work left undone, which causes other productivity problems. If employees believe they cannot request and receive time off, many of them do not even ask for it. They just call in sick. In essence, they plan to use sick time to meet nonwork needs.

According to the 2006 CCH *Unscheduled Absence Survey*, only 35 percent of all sick hours were used for personal illnesses. This means 65 percent of all sick time was used for reasons other than personal illnesses. In 1995, survey respondents reported 45 percent of all sick hours were used for personal illnesses. Thus, about 20 percent fewer sick hours are being used today by employees who are actually sick. This is a disturbing and costly trend for companies, especially those competing in the global economy.

Use or Lose Mentality

Most sick-leave policies unintentionally foster a use-or-lose mindset. We often hear managers complain that workers have an entitlement mentality about pay for time-not-worked benefits (e.g., sick, vacation, holiday). However, just look at company policies. Unintentionally, many companies actually foster the "use or lose" mindset.

Examples taken from company policy manuals include:
- You earn one day of sick time per month. Any time not used by Dec. 31 is lost.

- You receive 10 sick days a year. Time is granted on your anniversary date or Jan. 1 and must be used by your next anniversary date or by Dec. 31. Time not used is lost.
- You earn vacation time during your first year of employment that can then be used during your second year. However, the time earned in the first year must be used by the end of your third year. You will otherwise lose any unused, earned vacation time.
- You receive three personal days on Jan. 1. If you do not use the time by Dec. 31, you lose any unused personal time.

In these cases, employees interpret the company policy to mean use or lose. Why then should management be surprised that employees have an entitlement mentality? The good news is PTO can help end the entitlement mentality.

- *Many managers and employees feel sick time granted by the company (six to 12 days per year) is theirs to use.* Instead of looking at sick time as insurance, workers believe the time is theirs. Even some managers and HR professionals support this view. In contrast, WorldatWork supports the position that sick time is insurance and it is unacceptable for workers to use the time unless they are really sick. This is a different mindset and is fostered by PTO design.
- *Most companies have a policy that excessive unscheduled absences will result in disciplinary action.* Consequently, workers learn it is acceptable to take time off so they just fall below the disciplinary "radar screen." For many workers, this means they can take some additional sick time off with pay (even if they are not sick) and not have to worry about being disciplined.

In today's competitive marketplace, a company's fiscal viability is threatened by high costs associated with traditionally generous paid time off benefits. Therefore, reducing these costs is good business and good for employees.

What is a PTO Bank?

Traditionally, employees receive paid time off benefits (vacation, sick time, personal holidays, etc.) in separate accounts. Each time-off benefit has its own policies and practices. With PTO, employees receive a "bank" of time to be used for absences.

PTO banks usually include hours for vacations, sick time, personal holidays and, at times, legal holidays. Because of infrequent use and the possibility of adverse employee relations, PTO banks do not include time off for jury duty, military duty and bereavement leave. These benefits are administered by other company practices.

PTO costs are capped by limiting the amount of sick time placed in the bank and by capping the amount of PTO time that can accrue.

Report Card on PTO Banks

There is considerable evidence that PTO banks are gaining in popularity because they reduce levels of unscheduled absences. National surveys from various sources including Commerce Clearing House (CCH), U.S. Chamber of Commerce, Mercer Human Resource Consulting and WorldatWork all report increased use of PTO plans by companies in all industries. Supportive studies include the following:

- The 2006 CCH *Unscheduled Absence Survey* reported that 70 percent of respondents use PTO plans, up from 16 percent in 1991 (the first year of this national survey). Overall, the CCH *Unscheduled Absence Survey* has reported for 16 consecutive years (1991–2006) that respondents rated PTO as the most effective absentee control approach.
- A 2005 survey from the U.S. Chamber of Commerce reported that 28 percent of respondents use PTO plans, up from 20 percent in 1991. The percentage of PTO users in this survey is lower than that in other surveys because more than half the employers had less than 100 employees, and small companies tend not to use PTO plans because they offer low amounts of paid time off.
- A 2004 Mercer survey reported 42 percent of respondents use a PTO program, up from 30 percent in 2000.
- As mentioned earlier, according to a 2006 *WorldatWork Hot Topic Survey*, 33 percent of the 679 surveyed companies reported having a PTO bank system for their employees. Among the companies without PTO banks, 31 percent indicated they are considering implementing one.

How PTO Banks Affect Chronic Sick-Time Abusers

Every company has chronic sick-time abusers. These are workers who believe every sick day is to be used whether they are sick or not. And it is not unusual for these workers to have a Monday or Friday pattern of absences. PTO does not prohibit workers from using PTO for sick time. However, because the bank of time is the employee's, it forces workers to be more judicious about using PTO for absences. If chronic abusers of sick time do not change their behavior, they will end up using vacation time for an illness. That is not something these workers want, because they will have less time for vacations.

Costs of Unscheduled Absences Other Than Sick Pay

- *Replacement costs*. This includes overtime, additional straight time, use of outside temporary help or internal worker pools to perform the work of absent employees.

- *Supervisory time* spent finding replacements or time the supervisor spends doing the work of absent workers.
- *Lower productivity* of employees who have to do the work of absent workers besides meeting their own productivity standards. The extra workload can create morale problems.
- *Lost productivity* by workers who upon return to work have to catch up on work left either undone or done incorrectly while they were out.
- *Lost revenue and customer dissatisfaction* results when service quality deteriorates due to staffing shortages caused by absent workers. A further consequence is losing some customers who may decide to "quit" purchasing your products or services because of their dissatisfaction.

Calculating Full Cost of Unscheduled Absences

According to the CCH *Unscheduled Absence Surveys*, the average cost of sick time per employee from 1995 to 2005 ranged from $572 to $789. If you add 25 percent to 100 percent for replacement and other costs, the range would be $715 to $1,578.

The 2005 CCH survey reported an average of $660. Adding 25 percent to 100 percent would have made the range $825 to $1,320. Using the 2005 CCH range, the cost of unscheduled absences for a company of 1,500 employees would range from $1,237,500 to $1,980,000.

How PTO Banks Save Companies Money

The short answer is employees receive less traditional sick time in a PTO account than the average use of pre-PTO sick time. For example:

Under a pre-PTO policy, a company grants 10 sick days a year for employee use. The average annual use of sick time is seven days. If the company had 1,000 employees, on an annual basis, employees would use 7,000 sick days (seven sick days/worker x 1,000 employees).

With PTO, the company places five traditional sick days into the PTO bank. In this way, the company caps its annual use of sick time to be 5,000 days (five sick days/worker x 1,000 workers). This means the company has reduced use of sick time by 2,000 days (7,000 – 5,000). The actual reduction is fewer than 2,000 days (explained in the Chapter 5 discussion on fiscal analysis).

Employees who need more than five sick days will have to fund those payments with other PTO time (vacation or personal holidays).

The remaining five sick days (10 – 5) are placed in another account called CAT (catastrophic account), which is used for illnesses after an employee is out for more than five consecutive work days. (PTO and CAT accounts are further discussed in Chapter 5.)

A real problem for companies is employees who have a pattern of Monday or Friday absences. With PTO, the company only funds this costly behavior for up to five days (because PTO accounts include five traditional sick days). Afterward, the employee must use other PTO time (vacation or personal time).

Employees like to use sick time because, in many companies, if they do not use it, they lose it. With PTO, the time belongs to the employee. There is no glory in abusing your own time.

How PTO Banks Reduce Unscheduled Absences

PTO banks give employees an incentive to use paid time off wisely. For example, employees who generally average six to eight sick days a year will now have a reason to reduce unscheduled absences to no more than six days (presume the PTO bank has six traditional sick days). Employees will otherwise end up using vacation or personal time allotments for their time off.

With PTO, employees who have a slight headache may make a greater effort to report to work rather than take the time off as a sick day.

Problems with Traditional Rewards Programs

Rewards programs are usually easy to design, implement and communicate. It would seem, therefore, that companies should promote them. The main problem is that these plans often reward employees who already have good attendance habits. Consequently, companies end up spending money to "incent" workers who have already demonstrated a good attendance work ethic.

In contrast, employees with poor attendance habits tend not to change their behavior to receive traditional rewards. These workers value time off with pay when they want to take the time (the Monday/Friday syndrome). Further, plans that reward good attendance tend to encourage employees with bad attendance habits to manipulate the system which, unfortunately, can create bad feelings among good attendees who have to cover for absent employees.

For example, a company has a perfect-attendance rewards program. An employee misses receiving the reward because of one unscheduled absence. Another employee in the same department receives the reward. However, the employee who just missed it is very angry. It seems the co-worker who received the reward really was out sick one day (which would have disqualified the worker). However, the boss changed the record to show a vacation day, not a sick day. The boss and the co-worker are friends. This may not happen too often, but it does occur.

How Traditional Sick Leave Practices Encourage Sick-Time Abuse

Many companies have a "use or lose" sick leave approach. For example, a company's handbook states employees receive 10 sick days per year. Any sick time not used by Dec. 31 is lost. So what happens in December? The company has a December sick-time problem.

Some companies allow workers to carry over sick time and have a cap (e.g., 60 days). In this way these companies avoid the potential "use or lose" outcome. However, in many of these companies, employees still view annual sick time as an allotment of time to use (whether sick or not). Compounding the problem is management support for taking all sick time before disciplinary action for excessive absenteeism begins. Reference is made to the company's employee handbook that states the company "provides 10 sick days a year" or "you earn 10 sick days a year." Some managers' interpretation is the time is yours, so you can use it and disciplinary action begins after all sick time is used (even if sick time is used one day at a time in the Monday/Friday pattern).

In another example, an employee informs the manager on Monday about needing time off on Wednesday to handle a personal issue. The manager informs the worker that, according to the employee handbook, an employee must give his/her manager at least three work days of notice when requesting time off with pay. Because Wednesday is only two days from Monday, the request is denied. Guess what happens on Wednesday before the work shift? The employee calls in sick. The result is the worker gets the day off with pay (sick time) and the manager has a staffing problem to resolve.

Cost of Unscheduled Absence vs. Percentage of Unscheduled Absences

Percentages do not give the total cost picture. Let's say, according to national norms, unscheduled absences average 2.9 percent of productive time. You calculate your company's rate to be 2.8 percent. You conclude you are better than national norm and thus do not have a problem.

Let's look further:

• Being close to the national norm means you accept being average. For many executives, being average is unacceptable.

• By not including replacement costs, you are underestimating the full cost of unscheduled absences. From this author's research, replacement costs can average between 25 percent and 100 percent of sick-time expenditures. In some cases, replacement costs are higher than sick-time costs.

- Once the magnitude of unscheduled absence costs are fully known, the company can determine whether it has a problem or not.

How PTO Banks Increase Productivity without Increasing Costs

With a PTO bank, paid productive time increases as paid nonproductive hours decrease. For example, employees average five sick days per year. The average cost of one sick day (based on average salaries) is $200,000. Therefore, the total cost is $1 million for sick pay ($200,000 x 5). If the replacement cost averages 50 percent of sick pay, the total annual cost is $1.5 million ($1 million x 150 percent), and the average daily cost is $300,000 and not $200,000 ($1.5 million divided by 5).

With a PTO bank, the company reduces unscheduled absences by one day per worker per year. The company now spends $800,000 for sick pay ($200,000 x 4). It also increases productivity by $200,000 without increasing the budget (previous $200,000 paid for sick pay is now paid for time worked) and realizes a savings of $100,000 due to reduction of replacement costs. Let's examine these conclusions.

- The $1 million of sick pay is accounted as paid nonproductive time. The worker is getting paid but is not productive (at home and not working). Because PTO effected reduction of one sick day per year for each worker, the company moved $200,000 (cost of one sick day) from paid nonproductive time (worker at home) to paid productive time (employee at work) without increasing the budget.
- Because the company reduced annual use of sick time use by one day, the company does not need to spend as much for replacements. Replacement cost averages 50 percent of sick-time cost. Therefore, one less sick day means the company saved $100,000 (50 percent of cost of one sick day = $200,000).

Can PTO Banks Be Perceived as Unfair to Employees Who Have Chronic Health Problems?

With a PTO bank, employees would have had more sick time to use under the pre-PTO plan, and those with chronic health problems may end up using traditional vacation or personal time for an absence. Because these employees may need additional health-care services, coverage under the Family and Medical Leave Act of 1993 (FMLA) or short-term disability may need to be considered.

It is possible that chronic health problems can be controlled over time. When this happens, the same employees may see the PTO plan offers extra time that can be used for scheduled absences.

Unfortunately, companies can no longer afford the "cradle-to-the-grave" benefits of yesterday and still remain competitive. Although PTO is not a panacea for every worker, it offers many benefits for the overwhelming majority of employees.

What is PTO's Effect on Employee Morale?

Based on company feedback and results of national surveys, employees tend to like PTO banks. Acceptance usually occurs after the company adequately explains reasons for the conversion to PTO and how it benefits the company and its workers. Acceptance is enhanced as employees learn consequences from not controlling costs of unscheduled absences. This may take a year or two with PTO. Some employees may need time to believe PTO can be beneficial. Many employers report PTO helps with recruitment because applicants look favorably on companies that have PTO plans, especially if a former employer had one.

Most employees know who abuses company sick time, because good attendees often have to cover for absent workers. Consequently, employees applaud efforts by management to address abusers. Thus, PTO can be a morale booster.

Can PTO Be Used with FMLA and Workers' Compensation?

Companies can easily use PTO/CAT time when paying for absences due to FMLA and workers' compensation. Companies have employees use PTO for the first five consecutive days of absence for FMLA and workers' compensation. Time away from work in excess of five work days is charged to a CAT account. Depending on company policy, employees may be allowed to credit their PTO account for the first five days of absence from their CAT account (if any time is available) upon return to work.

How is PTO Time Used for Overtime Calculations?

Depending on company policy, PTO time may or may not be viewed as time worked for purposes of calculating overtime. The usual decision is for companies to follow past practices.

When to Use a Consultant

Internal HR professionals or a consultant can perform all the tasks necessary for the design and implementation of PTO. A key variable is the amount of time internal HR staff can devote to PTO and the level of comfort to tackle plan design and implementation issues. Therefore, HR professionals need to assess what they can do and what they prefer a consultant to handle.

Many companies use consultants to direct fiscal analysis and assist with the design of a cost-effective PTO plan. Consultants can be very helpful when introducing a PTO model to employee task forces. Employee upset can be expected. Therefore, experienced consultants can help address employee concerns. Once PTO design is finalized, HR staff often handles companywide communication of the PTO program. A consultant or HR staff can take responsibility to draft written communications such as PTO policies and procedures and employee handouts.

Are There Creative Ways for Employees To Have Scheduled Time Off?

Many employees complain about being unable to schedule time off. Managers highlight business pressures as the reason for the difficulty in accommodating time-off requests. Consequently, some companies feel PTO exacerbates the situation by giving workers even more paid time off that cannot be scheduled.

PTO by itself will not make scheduling easier. What is required is more creative thinking by management and workers. Traditional mindsets may need to be challenged and modified.

Examples include management requirements for:

- Vacations in blocks of one week
- Use of a full day or half day for a doctor's visit
- A maximum number of days an employee can use for a vacation at one time (e.g., two weeks)
- Use of paid time off only during certain time periods or months
- Paid time off requests based on advance notice of at least three to five work days.

Managers who believe in "command and control" have no problem with these requirements. These managers ask how work can be accomplished without clear and rigid work rules. Besides, these managers believe that giving workers flexibility on scheduling time off will cause havoc in meeting work output demands. Some people may feel these managers have a good argument. So why should companies change? Let's look at the opposing views.

If you believe employees need flexibility to balance work and nonwork pressures, how can you support "command and control" views? If you believe employees are attracted to and will remain with employers who support work-life approaches, how can you not advocate greater give and take in scheduling time off? These are philosophical issues, but they go to the heart of how effective PTO will be for companies.

The following are examples of how companies use PTO to modify scheduling systems. The result is a win–win outcome for management and workers.

Employees are allowed to take paid time off in the minimum time charged in the pay system (often 15 minutes). Examples include:

- Employee leaves work 30 minutes early to see a doctor or attend a child's school function.
- Employee arrives at work one hour late because of a doctor or veterinarian appointment.
- Employee leaves work 1.5 hours early on Fridays during the summer to get a jump on shore traffic, or leaves earlier during the winter to get to the ski slopes earlier.
- Employee arrives at work two hours late on Mondays during the summer or winter to enjoy the shore or ski slopes.
- Employee takes three consecutive weeks off for a European vacation.

With the described accommodations, employees often feel more supportive of the company and, in many cases, workers fulfill a full day's work even though they work less than a full day. These examples show the benefit to companies and workers. But corporate executives must support flexibility and accommodation, because some managers will resist.

Fulfillment of company business objectives is paramount. However, there is considerable latitude about how work gets down. Command and control may have worked in the past, but many surveys highlight the need for greater flexibility to help employees balance work and non-work pressures. PTO is the answer. But, PTO's effectiveness is predicated on top management's support to achieve PTO's full potential.

Fiscal Analysis 5

Number crunching is the spring-board to support PTO plan design. A critical part of the PTO planning process is to make the business case for your PTO design. In particular, you must show the cost justification of various plan components. By cost justification, we mean you will have to:

- Prove PTO plan will save the company money—if not the first year, then in the second year.
- Show first-year costs and justifying them as one-time conversion costs.

We recommend you work closely with your CFO. We further recommend the CFO explain the fiscal justification of the PTO plan to your company's CEO and other line executives as necessary. Having the "numbers person" support the PTO plan adds considerable credibility.

These next two chapters will:

- Provide a working definition of eight key terms.
- Explain eight key calculations that serve as a foundation for your analysis. To help you use the formulas, numbers are included to help you understand their use in your own company. The illustrations offer a clearer under-standing of how fiscal analysis greatly influences and eventually supports PTO design.
- Introduce new terms to highlight sick time that can be influenced by the PTO plan (Workable Sick Time) and sick time that PTO will not affect (Noninfluential Sick Time).
- Present a PTO design based on the results from the eight key calculations and the corporate philosophy that drives PTO process.
- Include a worksheet for you to use to calculate the numbers for your company.

Working Definition of Key Terms

Sick Time: Hours or dollars a company annually pays when employees call in sick (influential + noninfluential sick-time costs).

NonInfluential Sick Time: Sick time paid to employees for disabilities. These include payments for workers' compensation, FMLA, short-term disability and long-term disability. The time is called noninfluential because companies can expect employees to use the time. Therefore, noninfluential time can be viewed as a fixed cost, and PTO is not expected to cause it to be reduced.

Influential Sick Time: The opposite of noninfluential sick time. These hours can theoretically be influenced by PTO plan.

Replacement Costs: These hours and dollars are paid to cover the cost of providing work to replace absent employees. Payments can be made to current staff who have to work extra hours or to those providing temporary help from outside. Replacement costs also include the costs resulting from the inability to meet customer needs due to absent workers, the time management needs to invest to find replacements, and the loss in productivity.

Workable Sick-Time Cost: This is the cost of influential sick time and replacement costs. These costs are influenced by PTO.

Macro or Full Cost of Sick Time: This is the cost of all sick time: influential sick time, noninfluential sick time and replacement costs.

PTO Account: A bank of time employees can use regardless of reason. PTO usually consists of some traditional sick time, vacation time, personal holidays and often legal holidays.

CAT Account: A bank of time employees can use for absences due to personal illness of more than five consecutive work days. Some companies call this account IPA (Income Protection Account) or CII (Catastrophic Illness Insurance).

Eight Key Calculations
Calculation No. 1: Costs of Unscheduled Absences
What follows is a five-step approach to calculate costs of unscheduled absences.
Step 1—Determine the Cost of Sick Time Used
Ideally, we recommend you find the cost of sick time for the last five calendar or fiscal years. This information will give you sufficient data to project future costs if no changes are made in your absentee control programs. If you only have one year's data, then that is all you can use. The cost figures should be summarized by sick hours paid and the cost ($) of sick hours paid. To calculate costs of sick hours paid, we suggest that you multiply sick hours paid by the average hourly rate of covered employees. (See Figure 5-1.)

Covered workers are defined as employees who were on the payroll for the full calendar or fiscal year and were eligible for sick pay. Employees who were eligible for sick time but worked less than a full year are not included because their numbers may skew results.

Figure 5-1
Formula for Calculating Cost of Sick Hours Paid

Year	Sick Hours Paid To Covered Workers		Average Hourly Rate		Total Annual Cost
2003	107,927	x	$19.80	=	$2,136,955
2004	114,302	x	$20.00	=	$2,286,040
2005	124,980	x	$21.10	=	$2,637,078
2006	13,014	x	$22.15	=	$2,503,260
2007	103,630	x	$23.00	=	$2,383,490

Note: The cost of sick time in 2007 is $2,383,490.

Figure 5-2
Sick Hours Paid That Can Be Influenced with Revised Costs

Year	Sick Hours Paid		% Noninfluential Sick Time		Noninfluential Sick Hours	Average Hourly Rate		Influential (a) Sick Hours		Influential Cost (b)
2003	107,927	x	12%	=	12,951	$19.80	x	94,976	=	$1,880,524
2004	114,302	x	10.5%	=	12,002	$20.00	x	102,300	=	$2,046,000
2005	124,980	x	13.5%	=	16,872	$21.10	x	108,108	=	$2,281,079
2006	113,014	x	22.7%	=	25,654	$22.15	x	87,360	=	$1,935,024
2007	103,630	x	15.7%	=	16,270	$23.00	x	87,360	=	$2,009,280

(a) Influential Sick Hours = Sick Hours – Noninfluential Sick Hours For 2007: 103,630 (sick hours paid)
   – 16,270 (noninfluential sick hours) = 87,360 (influential sick hours)
(b) Influential Sick Hours Cost = Influential Sick Hours (a) x Average Hourly Rate
Note: Influential sick time cost for 2007 is $2,009,280.

Figure 5-3
Influential and Noninfluential Sick Time Costs

Year	Influential Sick Time		Noninfluential Sick Time		Total Cost of All Sick Time
2003	$1,880,524	+	$256,430	=	$2,136,955
2004	$2,046,000	+	$240,040	=	$2,286,040
2005	$2,281,079	+	$355,999	=	$2,637,078
2006	$1,935,024	+	$568,236	=	$2,503,260
2007	$2,009,280	+	$374,210	=	$2,383,490

Note: Total cost of all sick time for 2007 is $2,383,490.

Step 2—Determine the Amount of Influential and Noninfluential Sick Time for Each Year

We suggest you subtract sick hours used for various disability payments, which represent noninfluential time, from sick hours paid. In other words, management can expect workers to incur the difference of these hours (although actual numbers will vary) every year. Noninfluential time includes workers' compensation, short-term disability, FMLA and long-term disability. Revised sick hours paid that can be *influenced* and costs now appear in Figure 5-2.

Influential sick time in theory can be influenced by a company's absentee management program. Research shows PTO motivates employees to reduce unscheduled hours and increase "presenteeism." This in turn causes a reduction in influential sick time and replacement costs. A breakdown of influential and non-influential sick time costs is found in Figure 5-3.

Step 3—Determine Replacement Costs

Replacement hours are incurred by employees who perform absentees' work. As a guideline, replacement costs can range from 25 percent to 100 percent of sick time incurred. Again, try to obtain replacement cost data for up to five years, if available. If not, include what you can obtain.

Most companies have difficulty determining replacement costs. We know the cost is there, but quantifying it presents problems. For example, we know overtime is expended to cover for absent workers. However, most companies do not specify why overtime is used in their accounting systems. Only total overtime used is reported. However, if your company has such records, you can identify the cost.

Replacement costs include:

1. Regular time paid to part-time workers
2. Vacation or personal time, if employee has used all sick time
3. Outside temporary help
4. Use of internal temporary worker pools
5. Overtime hours

You may need to talk with your company's budget staff or ask line executives how much they budget for sick-time coverage. If all else fails, ask your CFO to project the percent of sick time used as replacement costs. (See Figure 5-4.)

Step 4—Determine Workable Sick Time Costs
(Influential Sick Time + Replacement Costs)

Workable sick time represents sick time that PTO could theoretically influence. The time appears in Figure 5-5.

Figure 5-4
Replacement Costs Using 85 Percent of Influential Sick Time

Year	Replacement Cost
2003	$1,598,445 (85% of $1,880,524)
2004	$1,739,100 (85% of $2,046,000)
2005	$1,938,917 (85% of $2,281,079)
2006	$1,644,770 (85% of $1,935,024)
2007	$1,707,888 (85% of $2,009,280)

Note: Replacement costs for 2007 were $2,009,280.

Figure 5-5
Workable Sick Time That PTO Can Influence

Year	Influential Sick Time Cost		Replacement Costs (85% of Influential Sick Pay)		Total Full Annual Cost of Sick Time
2003	$1,880,524	+	$1,598,445	=	$3,478,969
2004	$2,046,000	+	$1,739,100	=	$3,785,100
2005	$2,281,079	+	$1,938,917	=	$4,219,996
2006	$1,935,024	+	$1,644,770	=	$3,579,794
2007	$2,009,280	+	$1,707,888	=	$3,717,168

Note: In 2007, the annual workable sick time was $3,717,168.

Figure 5-6
Total 'Macro' Cost of All Sick Time Plus Replacement Costs

Year	Total Cost of Sick Time		Replacement Costs (Macro Number)		Total Annual Cost
2003	$2,136,955	+	$1,598,445	=	$3,735,400
2004	$2,286,040	+	$1,739,100	=	$4,025,140
2005	$2,637,078	+	$1,938,917	=	$4,575,995
2006	$2,503,260	+	$1,644,770	=	$4,148,030
2007	$2,383,490	+	$1,707,888	=	$4,091,378

In summary (Use 2007 Data)

Sick time cost: $2,383,490 (influential + noninfluential sick time)

Macro cost of sick time: $4,091,378 (sick time cost + replacement costs)

Workable sick time: $3,717,168 (influential + replacement costs)

Step 5—Calculate Macro or Full Cost of Sick Time.

We recommend you show top management the macro cost of all sick time (influential, noninfluential and replacement costs). Executives can then see the full cost of sick time (macro) and what part of it that PTO can impact (workable sick time). Macro sick time in this example is presented in Figure 5-6.

Calculation No. 2: Percentage of Unscheduled Absences

Percentage of unscheduled absences is determined as follows:

Divide sick hours used (excluding disability hours) by productive hours. Productive hours is defined as regular and overtime hours used by covered/eligible workers. Percentage of unscheduled absences appears in Figure 5-7.

Calculation No. 3: Cost of Unscheduled Absences per Worker

This is a useful statistic, especially when explaining the cost impact of unscheduled absences to managers and employees. The cost is calculated in four ways. Note the main variable in Figure 5-8 is whether or not you include replacement costs.

Your sick hours and sick pay can be compared against national norms. Unfortunately, these surveys do not include replacement costs. However, your real or full cost of unscheduled absences includes replacement costs, so we recommend you include them in your calculations when analyzing your company's experience.

With data from your sick time cost analysis, you can compare your unscheduled absence costs per employee and the percentage of unscheduled absences with national norms (CCH and U.S. Chamber of Commerce). Remember these national surveys do not include replacement costs.

It is always helpful to compare your experience against established national norms. The results can be used to help employees understand why you need to control absence costs, especially if your company's experience is more costly than the experiences reported in national surveys. Using previous data, we can calculate annual average sick hours, sick days and sick dollars expended per worker. (See Figure 5-9.)

We now want to calculate the average annual Workable Sick Time cost per worker. Remember, Workable Sick Time includes influential sick pay and replacement costs. This is your true or full cost of sick time, and the time PTO can affect. (See Figure 5-10.)

Figure 5-7
Percentage of Unscheduled Absences

Year	% of Unscheduled Absences
2003	6%
2004	5.9%
2005	6.4%
2006	5.7%
2007	6.1%

Figure 5-8
Calculation for Cost of Unscheduled Absences

Sick Hours Only
1) Divide sick hours paid by eligible workers.
2) Divide sick dollars paid by eligible workers.
Sick Hours + Replacement Costs
3) Divide sick and replacement hours paid by eligible workers.
4) Divide sick and replacement dollars paid by eligible workers.

Figure 5-9
Annual Average Sick Hours, Sick Days and Sick Dollars Expended Per Employee

Year	Sick Hours Used (a)	Sick Dollars Paid (b)	# Employees	Sick Hours per Worker	Sick Days per Worker	Sick $ per Worker
2003	94,976	$1,880,524	1,696	56	7	$1,109
2004	102,300	$2,046,000	1,705	60	7.5	$1,200
2005	108,108	$2,281,079	1,716	63	7.9	$1,329
2006	87,360	$1,935,024	1,680	52	6.5	$1,152
2007	87,360	$2,009,280	1,560	56	7	$1,288

(a) Sick Hours Used is calculated by subtracting noninfluential sick hours from sick hour paid as reported on Chart B. For 2007, sick hours paid was 103,630, and noninfluential sick hours paid was 16,270 (103,270 – 16,270 = 87,360)
b) Sick Dollars Paid is taken from Chart B.

Average annual sick hours per worker: Divide sick hours used by number of employees.

Average annual sick days per worker: Divide sick hours per worker by eight hours (normal work day).

Average annual sick dollars per worker: Divide sick dollars paid by number of employees.

Results for 2007 per worker are:

Average Annual Sick Hours: 56

Average Annual Sick Days: 7

Average Annual Sick Dollars: $1,288

Calculation No. 4: Cost of One Sick Day for All Workers

Using data from Calculation No. 3, the full cost of one sick day is determined by dividing the total annual workable sick time cost by the number of sick days. In 2007, the cost of one sick day was $531,024. (See Figure 5-11.)

Calculation No. 5: Cost Impact of Adding Traditional Sick Time in PTO and CAT Accounts

How to Decide Number of Sick Days to Accrue Annually in PTO and CAT Accounts

Because there is a high probability that these costs will occur annually, they can be viewed as fixed costs. The costs are deducted from employee CAT accounts. Actual hours are 10.4 (16,270 disability hours divided by 1,560 eligible employees, per Figure 5-2). For this example, we will equate 10.4 hours as one day.

The break-even point is the amount of expected influential sick time, presuming pre-PTO sick time usage remains the same. The belief is PTO will motivate workers to reduce use of unscheduled absences for time off needs and scheduled time off in advance to meet nonwork needs.

Depending on business reasons for implementing PTO, the number of traditional sick days can be six or fewer. In this example, the company decides to be aggressive and plans to grant four traditional sick days in PTO. The remaining six sick days (10 days–4 days) are placed in CAT account. (See Figure 5-12.)

Calculation No. 6: Cost Impact of Granting Some Unused, Earned Sick Time Upon Conversion to PTO

How to Decide Amount of Sick Time to be Placed (as a Lump Sum) in PTO Accounts upon Conversion to PTO

When PTO is implemented, all employees have zero earned PTO time. PTO time is earned on an accrual basis. Most companies grant 1/26 of the annual PTO allowance after every pay period worked (26 pay periods in a year). Some companies grant 1/12 of the PTO annual allowance after every month worked. Therefore, if an employee is ill shortly after PTO implementation, the worker may have insufficient time to pay for absences. This has implications for employee relations, because the absent worker may have been a good attendee for years and may have had a large bank of unused, earned sick time before PTO. Now, with PTO, this good attendee could end up losing—not getting paid, while the employee would have been paid under the pre-PTO plan.

Figure 5-10
True or Full Cost of Sick Time That PTO Can Affect

Year	# Employees Sick Time Cost	Total Workable	Average Annual Cost per Worker
2003	1,696	$3,478,969	$2,051
2004	1,705	$3,785,100	$2,220
2005	1,716	$4,219,996	$2,459
2006	1,680	$3,579,794	$2,131
2007	1,560	$3,717,168	$2,383

Average annual workable sick time cost per worker is determined by dividing the total workable sick time cost by the number of employees. In 2007, the average annual cost of sick time per worker was $2,383.

Figure 5-11
Full Cost of One Sick Day

Year	Total Annual Workable Sick Time Cost	# Sick Days	Cost of One Sick Day (8-hour day)
2003	$3,478,969	7	$496,996
2004	$3,785,100	7.5	$504,680
2005	$4,219,996	7.9	$534,177
2006	$3,579,794	6.5	$550,738
2007	$3,717,168	7	$531,024

Based on the fiscal analysis, the summary of annual sick time costs for 2007 is as follows:

1. Total macro or full cost of sick time	$4,091,378
2. Total workable sick time cost (influential sick time cost + replacement costs	$3,717,168
3. Average workable sick time cost per worker	$2,383
4. Cost of one sick day	$531,024
5. # sick days used	7
6. Average influential sick time cost per worker	$1,288

Some companies just accept this possible employee-relations situation. Other companies want to give workers who had balances of unused, earned sick time a cushion upon conversion to PTO. This means placing some unused, earned sick time into employees' PTO accounts. Once in the PTO bank, the time can be used for any reason, not just for illnesses.

Granting the time is an added cost because employees will receive payment for all unused PTO time upon termination. Employees could also cash out some time if the company has that option. Figure 5-13 offers two options to address this issue.

The more conservative approach (Option B in Figure 5-13) is only 68 percent of the cost of Option A. What is important is that the company used actual sick leave balances to help calculate the costs. Now it is up to management to decide which option is best as the company tries to balance concern for cost savings and employee relations.

If we take the projected savings from granting less sick time (four days instead of six days)—$1,062,048, and subtract total cost (Option B: $424,488), the projected savings for the first year is $637,560).

Calculation No. 7: Cost Impact of Cashing-Out Unused, Earned PTO Time

A growing trend is for employers to allow employees to cash out some unused, earned PTO time, either once or twice during the year. A common date is the beginning of December (to help pay for holiday shopping). Companies require employees to have a certain minimum balance of time after cashing out. Common end balances range from 40 to 80 hours.

Let's use 40 hours as the end balance for cashing out time. Using the demographics from employee sick-leave balances in Figure 5-13, we can conclude that 1,115 employees (130 + 232 + 289 + 267 + 197) would not be eligible, because they have fewer than 40 sick hours in their bank. Therefore, in theory, 445 workers (1,560 – 1,115) would be eligible. Offsetting the low number (445) is the addition of vacation and personal holidays. However, workers like taking time off for vacations and might not want to cash out the time.

Let's project 30 percent of 445 eligible workers (i.e., 134) elect to cash out some time, and the average is two days.

Cost of 2 days = $368 ($184/day).

Total cost = $49,312 ($368 x 134).

However, offsetting the $49,312 is a reduction of replacement costs.

Figure 5-12
Projected Annual Savings

Company's average annual use of sick days per eligible employee = 7 days (per Calculation No. 4).

Average annual use of unscheduled absences of at least 5 consecutive work days per eligible employee = 1 days.

Number of sick days to be placed in CAT = 6

Number of sick days to be placed in PTO = 4

Cost of one sick day = $531,024 (per Figure 5-11)

Projected annual savings is: $1,062,048 ($531,024 x 2 days)

Note: Number of days (2) are determined by subtracting 4 days (traditional sick days placed in the PTO account) from 6 days (break-even point). In this example, the break-even point (6 days) is determined by subtracting 1 day for long-term absences from 7 sick days (average annual use of sick days).

Figure 5-13
Possible Formulas for Deciding How to Place Up to Three Unused, Earned Sick Days into PTO Accounts at Time of Conversion

Note: Full day = 8 hours

Option A

Balance of unused, earned sick hours upon conversion to PTO	Number of sick days to be placed into PTO account
0–7	0
8–15	1
16–23	2
24+	3

Using this approach, the employee who has between 8 and 15 unused, earned sick hours will have one sick day placed into a PTO account.

Option B

Balance of unused, earned sick hours upon conversion to PTO	Number of sick days to be placed into PTO account
0–23	0
24–47	1
48–71	2
72+	3

Using this approach, the employee who has between 24 and 47 unused, earned sick hours will have one sick day placed into a PTO account.

Figure 5-13 Continued

One way to project the cost is to generate a computer printout giving the number of eligible/covered workers by sick-time balances. The report can be sorted by full-day increments of eight hours each. For example:

Sick Hour Balances	Number of Workers
0 – 7	130
8 – 15	232
16 – 23	289
24 – 31	267
32 – 39	197
40 – 47	125
48 – 55	45
56 – 63	77
64 – 71	47
72 – 79	44
80 – 87	23
88 – 95	59
96 – 103	15
104+	10
Total number of employees	**1,560**

You then add the number of employees who would receive different amounts of sick time according to your company's formula. You would then multiply the cost of one, two or three days by the number of employees who would receive the days by the average cost of a day.

For a company of 1,560 employees, where the average daily wage is $184 (8 hours x $23), the added cost would be (using the number of employees previously identified by sick hours balances):

Option A

Number of Workers		Days		Daily Wage		
232	x	1	x	$184	=	$42,688
289	x	2	x	$184	=	$106,352
869	x	3	x	$184	=	$479,688

Total Cost (Option A): $628,728 ($42,688 + $106,352 + $479,688)

Option B

Number of Workers		Days		Daily Wage		
589	x	1	x	$184	=	$108,376
169	x	2	x	$184	=	$62,192
151	x	3	x	$184	=	$253,920

Total Cost (Option B): $424,488 ($108,376 + $62,192 + $253,920)

The company is paying the workers, so employees will have less time to take off in the future. From a cash-flow basis, the company would end up paying the $49,312 sometime in the future, either when the employees takes the time off with pay or as payment upon termination. The variable is replacement costs. Less time off with pay means lower replacement costs.

Because the replacement costs average 85 percent, the actual cost of the cash-out is 15 percent of $49,312, which is $7,397.

We now subtract $7,397 from the earlier projected annual savings of $637,560 in the first year. The revised projected annual savings is now $630,163.

Calculation No. 8: Projected Annual Savings from PTO

We started with a projected annual savings of $1,062,048 (2 days @ $531,024 per day).

We then subtracted the cost of placing sick time of $424,488 into the PTO bank at the time of conversion.

We now subtract the additional cost of the projected cash-out ($7,397) and arrive at an annual savings of $630,163 during the first year of PTO.

When projecting the PTO impact, it is helpful to show two- or three-year projections. This can be very important, especially if first-year costs exceed projected savings. Because conversion costs are incurred only once, many companies show a savings in the second and subsequent years. (See Figure 5-14.)

Figure 5-14
Total Projected Annual Savings for First Two Years of PTO

Year 1: $ 630,163

+Year 2: $1,062,048 (no conversion cost)

Total: $1,692,211

Projected savings do not reflect expected benefits of increase in productivity (at no additional cost) because of increase in "presenteeism" (or decrease in unscheduled absences) and associated savings from reduction of replacement costs. These savings can be significant, as shown by Rockford Memorial Hospital's experience. (See Chapter 8.) Based on the fiscal analysis, we are now ready to design the PTO plan.

Designing the PTO Plan   6

T he following PTO design is based on sample 2007 data from Chapter 5 about Fiscal Analysis. For each plan component, it is important to be able to highlight cost or savings. In this way, decision makers can more easily follow the rationale for the plan. Key plan design features are boldfaced, as follows:

PTO Account: On an annual basis, employees will accrue the following time:

- Four sick days (based on the numbers used in Figure 5-12)
- Current vacation allowance
- Current number of personal days
- Legal holiday time, which will be deposited in a PTO account during pay period in which a legal holiday is observed.

The PTO cap is 150 percent of an employee's annual amount of PTO time. Employees will receive additional annual vacation time based on tenure, according to current company policy. The 150 percent was judged to be a way to allow employees to accumulate time for long-planned vacations. The company wants employees to feel PTO gives them flexibility, and being able to plan for special vacations is seen as fulfilling that objective.

CAT Account: On an annual basis, employees will accrue six days (based on calculation in Figure 5-12). The cap is 60 work days, which is the waiting period for long-term disability (90 calendar days).

At **conversion**, employees will receive a lump sum of unused, earned sick time from the pre-PTO sick-time account based on having the following balance of unused, earned sick time:

Balance of sick hours	Days
0 – 23	0
24 – 47	1
48 – 71	2
72+	3

Further discussion of how company arrived at this formula is explained in Figure 5-13, Option B.

Cash-Out: Employees will be able to cash-in unused, earned PTO time in November. Employees must have a remaining balance of five PTO days (40 hours) after cash-out. The justification for cash-out is explained in Calculation No. 7 in Chapter 5.

Debit/Credit CAT Alternative: An employee uses PTO time for the first five days of absence due to a personal illness. Afterward, an employee would use CAT for the remainder of the absence. An alternative—the Debit/Credit alternative—uses CAT hours for extended absence due to illness.

This is how the Debit/Credit provision works: Upon return to work after an extensive absence due to personal illness (more than 5 consecutive work days), the employee can charge the CAT account for the first five work days of absence (initially deducted from the PTO account) and credit the PTO account with the five CAT days. This presumes the employee has excess CAT time available upon return to work after the illness.

The rationale for this option is the high probability the employee's absence for illness (even with the required doctor's note) is valid. Why should the employee have to use PTO time (which is comprised of vacation, sick and personal time) for longer-term illnesses? This arrangement engenders good employee reaction to PTO and

---

Figure 6-1
Traditional Approach vs. Debit/Credit Alternative

CAT balance: 85 hours
PTO balance: 55 hours
Employee out sick for seven work days (7 days x 8 hours/day) = 56 hours

Traditional Approach

	PTO Account	CAT Account
	55 hours	85 hours
	40 hours (minus first 5 work days)	16 hours (minus 2 work days)
Balance:	15 hours	69 hours

Debit/Credit Alternative

	PTO Account		CAT Account
	55 hours		85 hours
– First 5 work days	40 hours	– 2 work days	16 hours
Balance:	15 hours		69 hours
Hours from CAT:	+ 40 hours	– 5 work days	40 hours
Final Balance:	55 hours		29 hours

Figure 6-2
Pre-PTO vs. PTO

	Pre-PTO Program	PTO Program
Vacation Time	10	0
Sick Time	10	0
Personal Time	3	0
Total	23	0
PTO Account	0	18
CAT Account	0	5
Total	0	23

helps support the view that PTO is fair and reasonable. It also highlights CAT's value.

Figure 6-1 illustrates the traditional approach versus the Debit/Credit alternative.

The annual CAT amount is the difference between the number of traditional sick days placed in a PTO account and the number of traditional sick days provided in the pre-PTO arrangement. Figure 6-2 shows configuration of a PTO program and compares it to a pre-PTO program.

Workers' Compensation: Employees must use PTO time as payment during the seven-calendar-day waiting period (five work days) of workers' compensation. After the seventh day of absence, CAT time is used for payments. Using the Debit/Credit alternative, after becoming eligible for workers' compensation, the employee will have up to five days taken from CAT account (if days are available) and credited to the PTO account. In this way, an employee will actually end up using CAT time and not PTO time for the waiting period.

FMLA: Payments for FMLA will be deducted from the PTO account. If the absence is for a personal serious health condition, the first five days are charged to the PTO account. All time after five days will be charged to the CAT account. Using the Debit/Credit alternative, after the fifth day of absence, up to five days will be deducted from the CAT account (if time is available) and credited to the PTO account.

Worksheet to Complete Fiscal Analysis for Your Company

Determine Cost of Unscheduled Absences
The first step is to determine total annual cost of sick hours paid for each of the last five years (if possible). If you have data for less than five years (e.g., three years), then use the data you have. Remember covered workers are defined as the number of employees who are eligible for sick time for the entire time period being evaluated. Ideally, average

hourly rate is defined as average hourly rate for covered workers. However, your management information system might not be able to generate this number. So, you may need to use average hourly rate for all workers eligible for sick time.

Year	Sick Hours Paid	x	Average Hourly Rate	=	Total Annual Cost
2003					
2004					
2005					
2006					
2007					

Calculate Amount of Influential Sick Time

Noninfluential sick hours represent time employees used for disabilities. These include: workers' compensation, short-term disability, FMLA and long-term disability. Management can expect some of these hours to be used every year. Therefore, a fixed cost of sick time is number of disability hours used. PTO will not necessarily reduce these hours. Therefore, we recommend you:

- First calculate what we call noninfluential sick time for each year in your analysis
- Subtract amount of noninfluential sick time from total annual sick hours used. This will give you amount of influential sick time (theoretically, this time can be controlled).

Year	Sick Hours Paid	Noninfluential Sick Hours	Revised Sick Hours Paid (a)	Average Hourly Rate	Total Annual (b) Influential Cost
2003					
2004					
2005					
2006					
2007					

(a) Total sick hours paid – noninfluential sick hours paid
(b) Revised sick hours paid x average hourly rate

Replacement Costs

Replacement costs are the hours used by workers who do the work of absent employees. These can be company workers who work extra hours or outside temporary help.

Year	Replacement Costs
2003	
2004	
2005	
2006	
2007	

Annual Cost of Workable Sick Time

You will add influential costs plus replacement costs to determine total annual workable sick time.

Year	Influential Sick Time Cost	Replacement Costs	Annual Workable Sick Time
2003			
2004			
2005			
2006			
2007			

Please note: *Annual workable costs* do not include *noninfluential costs*. These costs will probably be deducted from employee CAT accounts and, therefore, it is important to report *noninfluential costs* to top management. However, by separating noninfluential time from *annual workable costs*, you can more clearly show PTO's impact on reducing unscheduled absences.

Even though you have separated influential from noninfluential costs, you should show top executives what we call "macro" sick time costs because the figure includes influential, noninfluential and replacement costs.

'Macro' Sick Time Costs

Year	Total Annual Influential Cost	Noninfluential Costs	Macro Cost
2003			
2004			
2005			
2006			
2007			

PTO Design Features That Can Cause Employee Dissatisfaction

At benefits seminars, managers often ask for advice about PTO design features that cause employee dissatisfaction. These include:

1. A cash-out policy that pays less than 100 percent (for example, 50 percent or 75 percent).

2. Employees must use all PTO time by a certain date; unused, earned PTO time is otherwise lost.

3. PTO bank is used to pay for bereavement leave.

1. Cash-out policy of less than 100 percent value of PTO time

Some companies allow workers to receive cash for earned, unused PTO time, usually at the end of the year. A balance of PTO time is required (often five to 10 days) after cash out. These companies believe cash outs are cost-effective. Why then should employees be reimbursed for less than 100 percent value of each day, especially because the company pays 100 percent for unused, earned PTO time upon termination? No wonder employees become confused and upset. Workers feel the company is being unfair.

Some companies reimburse less than 100 percent to save money. However, there is a concept called the "wounded bear," in which affected workers feel somewhat cheated. Examples include a two-tier compensation approach where you pay new workers less than current workers in the same pay grade, grant fewer benefits to new workers than to current workers, or pay less than 100 percent for PTO time.

Suggested Alternative Companies implement PTO to save money, but the process impacts morale. Therefore, we suggest that you pay 100 percent for cash-outs. If you think it is too expensive, we suggest that you consider reducing the amount of time employees will be allowed to cash out—but at 100 percent value. You want workers to feel positive about PTO. Why give them a tangible reason to question management's intentions?

2. Employees must use all PTO time by a certain date. Unused, earned PTO time is otherwise lost

Companies grant PTO time to be used. Then why be surprised if employees become upset if company also says time must be used by Dec. 31 or you will lose it?

It is very difficult for employees to use all earned time by a certain date. Often, managers will not grant time off due to production issues. Sometimes, employees may wish to bank time for a longer scheduled vacation. And if companies insist on use or lose, there could be a shortage of workers at the end of the year because of paid time off. In these situations, present workers are often asked to work longer hours, which causes additional morale problems.

Suggested Alternative To avoid problems, we recommend you cap the maximum amount of PTO time that can be earned (e.g., 150 percent of the annual allotment). In this way, employees can carry over unused, earned PTO time. The cap provides companies with a safeguard, because unused time becomes more expensive over time (due to pay increases). If an employee reaches the cap, no additional time is added. However, the employee does not lose what has already been accrued.

Some companies allow workers to deposit PTO time in excess of the cap to their CAT accounts. Companies want to show workers the time is being credited to one of their accounts. The potential downside to this alternative is workers still need time off with pay. Therefore, most companies have internal controls to monitor PTO use and interact with managers who have difficulty scheduling workers with time off during the year. The goal is to find some creative cost-effective ways to schedule workers with some time off. In reality, we all need some periodic "R & R."

3. PTO time is used to pay for bereavement leave

Workers may feel it is unfair to use PTO time to handle and attend the funeral of an immediate family member. Companies rarely add time to PTO accounts for bereavement leaves because not all employees use the leave. Therefore, affected employees use traditional vacation time in PTO accounts.

Suggested Alternative To avoid morale problems at a very sensitive time (death of a family member), we recommend bereavement leave be administered per current company practice and not be included in the PTO plan.

Communication and Implementation Strategies 7

One of the most difficult and challenging aspects of PTO planning is employee communication. Although PTO has many positive features, some employees will not like it. There are four main reasons to expect resistance.

1. Workers receive less traditional sick time in PTO than in the pre-PTO arrangement.
2. Some workers feel they need a pre-PTO amount of sick days in addition to other paid time off benefits (e.g., vacation and personal time).
3. Some workers feel uncomfortable with change.
4. Some workers are suspicious of management's real intent.

Here are two approaches to explaining PTO:

Approach A: Tell employees about PTO. PTO is explained at the time of implementation.

Approach B: Review PTO with a group of employees *before* implementation to obtain their reaction to PTO. The key to this alternative is management's desire to listen to workers' comments and to be prepared to make some modifications, if appropriate.

Unlike Approach A, Approach B has active employee participation or input to PTO design and implementation. It provides opportunities for workers to have influence on PTO planning,

The decision to use one of these options will be based on company culture and management style when implementing new programs.

Many companies opt for Approach A and elect to just "tell the workers." These companies believe convening a task force before implementation will cause problems. Executives are worried that workers may not like PTO. They believe employees may spread rumors that will cause workforce upset, ask for additional benefits, ask for changes and/or cause delay in implementation.

Therefore, executives who support Approach A believe it is best just to tell workers. As one CEO told the author, it is management's job to come up with solutions and to then tell workers. Good management, though, means also controlling any possible upset.

Executives who favor Approach B believe workers react more favorably to change before implementation if they have:

- An opportunity to understand why management is making the change
- Time to think about the new program
- The chance to receive answers to their questions.

Although employees may be upset with PTO, the belief supporting Approach B is that it is best to talk through problems with workers before implementation than to have to handle a crisis due to adverse employee reaction due to misunderstanding after implementation. It is like the Pennzoil commercial: "Pay me now or pay me later."

Executives who support Approach B believe the dialogue gives employees time to consider and understand management's reasons for converting to PTO; in particular, it gives them an opportunity to find out how PTO benefits workers and the company. The meetings also give employees a chance to offer ideas that, in many cases, have enhanced the quality of PTO plan without adversely affecting management's objectives.

While there are risks with Approach B, companies that support this option believe that:

- PTO reflects a different way of thinking about pay-for-time-not-worked benefits. Therefore, interaction with employees is necessary to help workers understand the company's rationale for PTO and offset any potential difficulties, especially those due to misunderstanding or the rumor mill.
- The dialogue helps to avoid problems rather than cause them. By airing concerns, management has the opportunity to "set the record straight." At least management knows what the concerns are and has a chance to address them before implementation.
- PTO is a good benefit and responds to today's business and employee needs.
- Any potential upset is best handled before implementation rather than after it, when damage control is the only option.
- Employees react more favorably when management engages them in dialogue rather than communicating via memo or e-mail that closes the door for comments before implementation.
- Executives have a better chance for employee task force members to support management with implementation because of the time the company spends on informing and listening to them. They agree with the concept that "people support what they help to create."
- Conversion to PTO is similar to implementation of a new company product or

service. Companies often delay implementation or modify new product/service due to customer concerns which are identified during the "test marketing" of the new product/service. The same logic applies to PTO.

How *Not* to Implement a New Benefits Program

A Fortune 500 company announced it was terminating an important benefits plan and replacing it with an alternative plan that was less costly to the company. Employees were informed of the change via e-mail and an internal Web site. No employee meetings were held. The written communication highlighted benefits to the company. The company stated how the plan would save it $200 million per year. Unfortunately, the company did not make it easy for workers to understand the impact of the conversion. The lack of candid or clear communication increased employee confusion because it caused workers to begin to wonder about how adversely the change would affect them.

In response, company employees figured out the impact themselves. Many workers were angry when they discovered they would lose a considerable part of the coverage they currently enjoyed. Because the company had made it very difficult for employees to obtain accurate information, employees began communicating among themselves via their own Web site.

The adverse employee reaction (which became known as an "employee revolt") caused management to eventually modify its position. The company ended up spending more than it had hoped to save. It also sustained significant damage to its image with workers and the public, and the federal government became involved due to possible disparate impact (unintentional discrimination) against a class of workers.

The communication strategy of telling employees about the new benefits plan created a nightmare for the company. The nightmare included having HR identified as the scapegoat in the mainstream media: "HR cannot hold up a conversation on the topic of calculating anything. They are more like used-car salesmen trying to sell a car with a sawdust filled transmission."

We now ask this question: How many companies would introduce a new product or service without asking a group of paying customers for their reactions? The answer? Very few, if any. We know the reason why this is the case, and it dates back to lessons learned from Ford Motor Co.'s introduction of the Edsel.

In the late 1950s, Ford Motor Co. introduced what it believed would be "the car of the century"—the Edsel. Unfortunately, customers did not purchase it. Consequently, Ford lost more than $260 million (a lot of money at that time). Ford never asked customers for their opinions. Ford thought it knew what customers wanted. The rest is history.

The Ford Motor Co. and the Fortune 500 company examples buttress our position of support for open communication with employees rather than a command-and-control style when communicating PTO to workers. Therefore, we recommend the following steps when designing your communication strategy (before announcing the PTO implementation date):

1. Prepare your PTO plan by researching current practices, as well as approaches covered in this guidebook.

2. Hold an information-gathering meeting with a cross-section of company managers:
   a. Explain the PTO plan to them.
   b. Ask them to list all the questions and concerns they feel employees, particularly "swing people" (informal leaders or opinion leaders in the company who are influential nonmanagers), will have about the plan. Use the information provided in this meeting to prepare for the next two meetings with swing leaders.

3. Plan to have at least two meetings with swing leaders:
   a. At the first meeting, explain the PTO plan to them, including why the company decided to adopt a PTO plan. Highlight how it will benefit the company and workers. Make sure they clearly understand how PTO will differ from your pre-PTO paid for time not worked benefits—even if it means some employees may receive less time. We have found it is best to be candid up front. If you are not candid, workers will eventually get the facts and then you have to do damage control.
   b. Ask them for their reactions to and questions about the proposed plan. Write their views on a pad of paper on an easel so everyone can see the comments. Swing people are not shy and will give you comments—some you may not want to hear. Listen to their opinions without being judgmental. Be prepared for swing leaders to be frank and open about their concerns.
   c. If there is time at this meeting, respond to questions and address concerns. If the meeting lasts more than an hour, ask the attendees to come to a second meeting to continue the discussion.

4. In the interim, HR professional should review employee views with top executives and decide how to respond. Having executive support of any modifications is important before second meeting with swing people.

5. Hold the second and final meeting with swing leaders:

   a. Explain any modifications to the plan and reinforce, if necessary, plan components that remain unchanged. Address all concerns at this time.

   b. Gather any additional feedback offered by swing leaders.

   c. The second meeting usually produces closure. However, subsequent meetings may be necessary based on the HR professional's assessment of employees' acceptance of the PTO plan and the value to continue discussion to address open issues.

6. Use the information gleaned to help prepare the communication strategy. Open dialogue with employees, as well as command-and-control style both have risks.

However, what company wants to be known for introducing the second Edsel?

Moving from Command-and-Control to Greater Employee Participation

A highly respected company of 6,500 employees hired a consultant to assist with PTO planning. The consultant's approach included interaction with a group of swing people. The company spent six months designing a PTO plan. It was time to obtain feedback from employees. Just prior to the first meeting, the consultant was told the CEO had problems with sharing PTO information with employees before the plan was finalized.

Company culture supported top management making critical decisions and then telling workers about the change. The consultant's approach (which the company agreed to in the original proposal) countered the corporate leadership style.

The CEO was worried about the risks of sharing information with employees before the PTO plan was finalized. This top executive feared:

- The rumor mill might be flooded with false information and thereby cause employee upset.
- Employees might not like the PTO program and demand changes.
- Implementation might be delayed.
- More work might be required.

The consultant emphasized the risks of not "testing" the PTO program with a group of swing people. Companies test new products and services with a group of paying customers before actual implementation, the consultant argued, so why should testing PTO design be any different?

Company executives understand the merits of testing new products or services before implementation and, if necessary, making changes—even costly ones—if doing so makes sense. However, reviewing a proposed benefits change was viewed differently. In reality, there is no difference between testing a new benefits change with employees and testing a new product or service with a group of paying customers.

After much discussion, the CEO agreed to a modified review of the PTO plan. The CEO allowed middle managers to meet, instead of nonmanagement swing people, and called the sessions "town meetings."

At the sessions, a 30-minute PowerPoint presentation explained the PTO plan. Afterward, managers formed groups of 10 and were asked to identify features they liked about the plan and the challenges presented by it. Examples of their replies follow.

Features Liked About PTO

- Provides flexibility
- Rewards workers who do not abuse sick time
- Simplifies record keeping
- Enables managers to plan for scheduled absences
- Permits buy-back of unused time
- Helps managers better manage time
- Remedies the "crunch" of time off so workers will not lose vacation time
- Is easy for employees to understand
- Appears fair to all
- Offers privacy in scheduling time off
- Discourages employees to lie about being sick
- Considers work and life issues
- Allows for a fair conversion of existing leave
- Encourages short-term planning and use of paid time off
- Supports appropriate management of time
- Acts as a good recruitment benefit
- Proves to be a better benefit than U.S. Savings Bond for perfect attendance.

Challenges Presented by PTO

- Employees who use 12 sick days a year will lose a benefit
- Misunderstanding of "entitlement" versus benefit
- Granting additional time off during tight labor situations
- Why only grant 75 percent of day's wages when cashing out PTO day?
- Balancing use of PTO and adequate coverage of work areas

- Need to clarify existing rumors
- Short amount of time to educate workers
- Increased managerial responsibilities
- Perception of long-term workers—time off is an "entitlement"
- Workers who report to work when sick
- What happens to accruals when employees reach PTO cap?
- Major change especially for long-term workers (who are the company's backbone).

After reviewing both positive features and challenges, managers met to decide next steps. The managers recommended the following:

1. Convene a managerial task force to look for innovative ways to schedule time off. Managers felt that current paid time off practices were too rigid and that many employees had difficulty taking time off. With PTO, many workers will have additional time to use; therefore, it will be important to have more effective ways to schedule time off.

2. Management decided to pay 100 percent of a day's wages when cashing out PTO days instead of the initial rate of 75 percent of a daily wage.

3. Because of the town meetings, managers felt "we're all in this together" (lifeboat analogy). The discussions helped managers better understand why the company was implementing PTO and how the PTO plan would benefit both the employer and employees. Now the challenge was to help employees understand what the managers now know.

4. Need to give employees facts and figures of costs of unscheduled absences when explaining PTO to all workers. Managers believed if employees understood the costs to the employer and consequences of unscheduled absences, they would be more receptive to PTO.

5. Important to highlight how PTO will help employees meet family and personal obligations.

6. Use question-and-answer format when explaining PTO in an employee handbook. Managers' comments identified issues that the PTO task force was able to address. As a result, the employee meetings went very well. The managers' support assisted in worker acceptance of PTO.

The CEO also learned a valuable lesson. Managerial/employee feedback does not have to be feared. It can actually help. It is the same lesson Ford Motor Co. learned with the Edsel.

How to Introduce PTO to a Group of Employees

When explaining a PTO program for the first time, it is very important for the speaker to be perceived as credible. The speaker needs to be well prepared to:

- Succinctly explain why the company decided to convert to a PTO plan
- Describe plan components
- Explain how the plan will affect workers—positively and perhaps negatively.
- Answer "tough" questions.
- Keep the message simple so it is understood by the audience.

Opening comments set the meeting's tone. The following is an example of an introduction:

"Thank you for coming. We're here to explain a new program you might have heard about. It's called PTO. PTO is a different way for you to earn and take paid time off.

We are changing to PTO because of the high cost of unscheduled absences. You might be surprised to learn that in the past five years, costs of unscheduled absences have grown considerably. By unscheduled absences we mean those absences that occur when employees are scheduled for work and are unable to report to work due to personal illnesses or other personal reasons. The absences negatively affect our ability to be competitive, which impacts your job security. Last year we spent more than $3 million for sick pay and necessary replacement costs. This is $250,000 more than what we spent the previous year. And we expect costs to continue to go up if nothing changes. These costs hurt us as we try to provide a competitively priced product.

On the other hand, we realize workers need paid time off to address personal and family needs. Many employees have told us about the difficulty of balancing work and nonwork pressures. Getting time off when needed for personal and family obligations is very important.

We believe PTO will help the company save money and give you the paid time off and the flexibility you want and need.

As we explain how PTO works, please keep the following in mind:

1. No one will lose any paid time off earned prior to conversion to PTO.
2. The change to PTO is being driven by our desire to remain a viable competitive company.
3. It is very important to management that all of us have a system that gives us flexibility to meet personal and family obligations.
4. PTO is a different way of thinking about how to earn and use paid time off.
5. PTO is growing in popularity in all industries throughout our country. Workers in all companies have needs that are similar to ours. And PTO is reported in surveys to be helpful in meeting those needs well.

How Change Theories Give Guidance for PTO Implementation

PTO is the end result of a change process. Therefore, by reviewing change theories and concepts, HR professionals will gain understanding of why resistance occurs and how to effect a successful conversion to PTO. The key is not to avoid resistance but to manage it well.

The primary change theory we will use was advanced by Kurt Lewin more than 50 years ago. Lewin has been cited as the founder of modern social psychology. Lewin's model is known as *"unfreeze-change-refreeze"* theory and serves as a theoretical model for many other change concepts.

Lewin concluded that successful change (individual or group) is the result of a dynamic human process. The first phase begins with an *unfreezing action*. This occurs from dissatisfaction with a present activity. With PTO, the company feels current paid time off practices result in a competitive disadvantage that cannot be continued. Also, employees need assistance to better balance work and nonwork pressures. Therefore, top management decides a *change* is necessary to address the dissatisfaction. With PTO, the change results in a PTO program for the company. The final action is called *refreezing*, which enables the company and workers to return to equilibrium or certainty.

People generally dislike the uncertainty that occurs whenever change becomes a strong possibility. Humans like to operate in a personal comfort zone that gives security. When our security is threatened (by a change), we often become defensive and tend to resist moving outside of our comfort zone. Just look at resistance to modifying Social Security. Based on projections, the federal government will have a major problem living up to promised benefits. Many articles have been written by well-respected experts acknowledging need for reform or change. Yet it is the rare politician who will propose a significant change, due to the expected adverse reaction from voters. This is why Social Security has been called the "third rail of politics." Another way of describing the resistance is to note that people are more fearful of the ramifications from any change than of the consequences of not changing.

Not surprisingly, Lewin found that with change one can expect resistance. Lewin further explained resistance as the result of a group or individual experiencing the feeling of being "out of equilibrium" due to change forces. The resistance is the group's reaction to regain the "known" equilibrium. According to Lewin, the key to successfully overcoming resistance is finding ways to reduce the causes of the resistance (or as Lewin would say, the "restraining forces"). Applying Lewin's lessons to PTO conversion, the author has found that the influence of restraining forces will be reduced by helping those affected (employees) to understand:

1. Why change is necessary, including a discussion of the consequences of not changing
2. Why the change is in the best interest of workers and the company
3. How to reap comparable or even better benefits with PTO.

The following change concepts further clarify why you can expect resistance to change and what management can do to address expected resistance.

Why You Should Expect Resistance to Change

- Employees are not resistant to change, but old habits die hard.
- People with a vested interest in the way things are will be upset when you change them.
- The difficulty is not with new ideas but in escaping old ones.
- Change represents the unknown; that is why it is often viewed with suspicion.

What Management Can Do to Address Resistance

- If you can change the way employees think, then you have a chance to change the way they behave.
- Give workers impacted by PTO a viable alternative to their current paid time off benefits.
- Significant change rarely occurs in the absence of economic pain. Therefore, help those affected by change to understand why it is in their best interests to shift gears (accept change).

The first grouping of sayings (why expect resistance to change) highlights the impact of our personal values and habits. For example, about 80 percent of Americans annually invest more than $2,200 and are guaranteed a loss. And, if you try to persuade them to change their investment, they will think you are crazy. What am I talking about? Tax refunds!

In recent years, the average tax refund was a little more than $2,200. Refunds are actually an overpayment of taxes. In essence, Americans end up giving the federal government an interest-free loan. You have to pay taxes, but why be overly generous? The reason: it is a forced savings—a habit!

What Americans lose by this "forced savings" is the full purchasing power of their tax refunds. The money returned can purchase less than when it was earned. The reduction in purchasing power is due to inflation. What's amazing to me is that many of the workers who complain about the high cost of benefits and the need for higher wages have no problem losing part of the purchasing power of their money.

People have the right to spend their money however they want. But the facts about how many people treat tax refunds show the influence and possible consequences of our personal habits and beliefs. By the same token, employees are used to their time off benefits and have planned time off based on the current arrangement. Some companies grant time off before it is earned. In this way, employees who enjoy skiing can take time off during the beginning of year, since the company up-fronts time for employee use. When you tell workers that the company is converting to an accrual system (earn 1/26 of annual allotment every pay period instead of receiving an annual amount in a lump sum), you can expect resistance. Workers are going to ask: "How will I be paid for my annual winter or summer vacation?"

So what can we learn from this example? The antidotes are explained in the second grouping of sayings.

With tax refunds, employees begin to modify their behavior as they learn the fiscal consequences of overpaying taxes and the benefits of a 401(k) plan. This awareness usually occurs after attending financial educational programs that many companies sponsor.

With PTO, ways to cause employees to open their minds to consider another way of thinking about paid time off benefits are as follows:

1. Show workers PTO's benefits as explained in the communication section of this guidebook.

2. It is important that workers see that they will receive the same paid time off annual allotment they received before, and that they will receive it in two accounts (PTO and CAT) instead of the traditional accounts of sick, vacation, personal time and legal holidays.

3. Many companies introduce cash-out provision as another benefit of PTO approach. Long-term employees who have more generous vacation allowances may look favorably on being able to receive some extra cash while less tenured workers may value time off with pay.

4. The Debit/Credit option engenders a feeling of fairness and has been well received by workers.

5. Workers need to understand the costs of unscheduled absences and why it is in the best interest of the company and employees to control the costs. One way to increase "scheduled absences" is by reducing the need for "unscheduled absences." Workers often call in sick when they are unable to receive a desired day or partial day off. Companies with PTO have cited how more timely communication between managers and employees have achieved an increase in "presenteeism" by reducing the need for unscheduled absences.

6. Work with a group of "swing people" (influential nonmanagers) as way to actively involve employees in the change process.

Change concepts are more than just theories. Their power is to help HR professionals understand the dynamics of change and to provide guidance about what is needed to effect a successful conversion to PTO.

Case Study:
Rockford Memorial Hospital

8

An example of PTO's impact is illustrated by using Illinois' Rockford Memorial Hospital's experience with PTO. Rockford Memorial Hospital is a 396-bed tertiary care hospital that is the flagship of the Rockford Health System, the largest health-care system serving Northern Illinois and Southern Wisconsin. The System has more than 70 primary care and specialty physicians in 15 specialties and a Visiting Nurse Association that provides home care visits in the region.

Rockford implemented PTO in 1993. Prior to PTO, Rockford was experiencing high unscheduled absences among its workforce of 3,300 employees. The absences were creating fiscal concerns and created employee morale problems because good attendees had to cover for those who were absent. Figure 8-1 shows PTO's impact on decreasing unscheduled absences from 1992 through 2005. The 1992 data is pre-PTO and is used as a benchmark (data not available from 1997 to 2000).

The percentage of unscheduled absences is calculated by dividing unscheduled hours by regular hours worked.

You will notice unscheduled absences decreased by 34 percent after one year of PTO (from 4.25 percent in 1992 to 2.81 percent in 1993). What is most

Figure 8-1
PTO's Impact on Decreasing Unscheduled Absences

Year	% of Unscheduled Absences
1992 (Pre-PTO)	4.25%
1993	2.81%
1994	2.71%
1995	1.89%
1996	1.81%
2001	1.17%
2002	1.16%
2003	1.11%
2004	1.04%
2005	1.21%

impressive is that the percentage of unscheduled absences continued to decrease over 13 years (1993–2005). The 2005 data, compared to that for 1992, shows a decrease of 72 percent (4.25 percent in 1992 versus 1.21 percent in 2005).

Other examples include a health-care system of 5,500 workers and a municipal transportation company of 2,000 employees. After implementing PTO, the health-care system's unscheduled absences were reduced by 25 percent while the transportation system experienced a 24 percent deduction.

Another way of understanding PTO's impact at Rockford is to view the increase in "presenteeism" (attendance). This means that employees are working and getting paid instead of not working (e.g., being at home after calling in sick) and getting paid.

Rockford increased full-time employees by 42 per year during the first four years of PTO. The increase resulted from a decrease in unscheduled absences. This means that Rockford increased its full-time equivalent workforce by 42 workers per year without increasing its budget. And Rockford lowered expenses due to lower replacement costs (not having to pay for additional staff to cover for absent workers). Employee morale increased because more staff was available to meet work demands.

Companies in all industries (as reported by surveys) are implementing PTO plans because they want to reduce unscheduled absences. In addition to paying sick time, companies experience replacement costs and customer dissatisfaction because work is unfinished or not done correctly by replacements. In addition, they face the costs of finding and paying for replacements.

Replacement costs can average 25 percent to 100 percent of actual sick-time paid. This means that if a company pays $2 million a year for sick time, the actual total cost could range from $2.5 million to $4 million. This does not include indirect costs associated with lost productivity and staff paid to find replacements. Although it is unusual, in some situations, replacement costs are actually greater than sick time paid.

Rockford reduced replacement costs (used to pay workers to do the work of absent workers) by $741,660 from 1993 to 1995. This resulted from a reduction of $391,660 in overtime and a $350,000 savings due to less temporary help needed from internal and external pools. Also during this time, the increase in attendance (employees were at work getting paid instead of being at home getting paid) saved Rockford an additional $3.5 million. This is how Rockford was able to increase full-time equivalents by 42 per year without increasing its budget.

Steps to Implement PTO

1. Identify business reasons for change

In the early 1990s, Rockford realized its sick-time policies were creating a fiscal problem. Unscheduled absences were increasing. Also, unused, earned sick time could be carried over year to year to a maximum of 1,300 hours. Workers with more than 480 unused, earned sick-time hours (there were many of them) received cash for all hours in excess of 480 upon termination. The "booked liability" was more than $1.5 million and was growing. These policies were not supporting the current business environment. The escalating paid time off costs were seen as threatening the hospital's competitive position. Rockford viewed PTO as the vehicle to use to address its business concerns while responding to workers' needs for paid time off to take care of personal and family obligations.

2. Identify full cost of unscheduled absences

The full cost of unscheduled absences includes sick-time and replacement costs. CCH and the U.S. Chamber of Commerce annually report sick-time costs. However, neither study deals with replacement costs. Calculating these costs takes time, because the accounting systems of most companies do not have a line item labeled "unscheduled absence replacement costs." Therefore, costing out the "full cost" of unscheduled absences gives a clearer picture of the consequences of unscheduled absences.

One client, a visiting nurse agency, thought it had a manageable absentee situation. After adding lost revenue (nurses bring in money for each home visit) to the cost of sick pay, the CEO saw a completely different picture—a significantly more costly one.

3. Conduct a detailed fiscal analysis to help determine the amount of traditional sick time that should be placed into PTO accounts.

Most companies place the current amount of vacation, personal/floating holidays into PTO, while some companies include legal holiday time. However, the key variable is the amount of traditional sick time to be placed into PTO. Companies tend to pay employees for unused, earned vacation, personal time and legal holidays upon termination. In contrast, unused sick time is not paid upon leaving the company. Because not every worker is replaced when absent, the granting of sick time in a PTO account could be viewed as increasing costs.

My style is to conduct the analysis with the active involvement of the CFO or designee and the HR executive. The goal is to have the CFO validate the fiscal integrity of the PTO plan to the CEO. In essence, having the top numbers person support PTO's fiscal soundness to the CEO lends considerable weight to the proposal.

4. Finalize proposed PTO plan

With the completion of step 3, management should be able to determine the number of paid time off hours for PTO accounts. As mentioned earlier, the key variable is the amount of traditional sick-time hours to be included in PTO banks.

Some companies decide to place the annual average number of sick days used per worker into individual employee PTO accounts. Other companies that are looking to save additional money will place a number of days that is less than the average use of sick days.

Before PTO, Rockford granted employees 12 annual sick days. With PTO, Rockford placed six traditional sick days (current annual average use of sick time) into an employee's PTO account together with the employer's past-practice amounts of annual vacation and personal holidays. The remaining six traditional sick days were placed into the employee's CII (Catastrophic Illness Insurance) account. CII is another name for CAT account. CII hours are used if the employee has been out of work for at least five consecutive work days due to a personal illness and needs additional time off.

Employees earned PTO and CII hours on an accrual basis. The cap for PTO is 150 percent of an employee's annual PTO allotment (the actual cap varies due to different amounts of annual vacation time that accrue in employees' PTO accounts); CII's cap is 60 days (the waiting period for long-term disability). Upon termination, employees are paid for all unused, earned PTO time. CII hours are not paid out.

5. Have top management support the proposed PTO plan

Top management should be apprised throughout the PTO planning process about how things are going. With the ongoing communication, executives have opportunities to have their questions answered and to think about reasons for design features. This makes obtaining final approval from top executives for PTO plan components easier, especially since there is less chance of "surprises."

6. Have a group of 'swing people' review the proposed PTO plan

All companies have "swing people." These are influential nonmanagement workers who command considerable respect among employees. Politicians refer to these employees as centers of voter influence. The group of swing people is your "test group" and should represent a cross section of your workforce.

Sharing information with swing people can be viewed as risky. For example, what happens if swing people object to PTO, create rumors or want further changes?

Swing people will be candid, because they are generally not afraid to speak their minds. So why should management subject themselves to possible cross-examination? There are good reasons. For example:

- You want to know employees' reactions—even if they are negative. It is better to know what you are up against before you implement PTO than to have to do damage control after PTO is implemented.

- Feedback gives management a chance to make modifications in response to employees' views before implementation rather than afterward.

- Your goal is to have swing people understand why you are implementing PTO, understand how it will impact and benefit the company and workers, and be aware of consequences to the company and workers if costs of unscheduled absences are not reduced.

- Switching to PTO can create resistance. PTO requires a different way of thinking about paid time off benefits and will mean some workers will end up having less time off than they did with pre-PTO benefits. Therefore, the key to a successful transition is how you manage the "pain of change."

If swing people accept PTO as a viable alternative to current paid time off practices, then implementation goes much smoother. There is a lower probability of workforce upset because employees often heed swing people's comments. Swing people often assist management with implementation, because they understand reasons for the change and why it makes sense. It is not easy to persuade swing people to support management. It takes time and preparation, but the end result is worth the effort.

You may need two or three meetings with swing people. At the first meeting, you explain reasons for the change, describe PTO design, and highlight its impact. You then ask for reactions. You can expect objections and sometimes the discussions may get heated. A follow-up meeting should be scheduled two weeks later to continue the discussion and to provide management's responses to workers' concerns. In the interim, management can consider employee reactions and possible plan modifications. Workers also have time to think about PTO—now armed with facts.

At Rockford, a hospital spokesperson explained (with numbers) the high cost of the current absentee program and how expenses negatively threatened the hospital's welfare. In essence, workers received new information that helped many of them to understand why the fiscal imbalance produced by the cost of unscheduled absences had to be addressed. If it were not addressed, the hospital and employees could suffer negative consequences. Employees also learned how the hospital gets paid for its services and the consequences of lower reimbursements from third-party payers. For many workers, this was the first time they had heard a candid explanation of health-care finances. It was an eye-opener.

Some of the swing people liked what they heard. Others had some misgivings. In particular, two issues of concern surfaced:

1. Why was the hospital planning to discontinue sick-time payout upon termination?

2. Why will employees have less sick time with PTO than they had before?

It is not unusual when presenting changes (even if changes make sense) for those affected to initially focus on why not to change. As Machiavelli stated in *The Prince*, "There is nothing more difficult to carry out or more doubtful of success or more dangerous to handle than to initiate a new order of things." Someone else stated, "Expect resistance and be prepared to deal with it. People with a vested interest in the way things are will be upset when you change them." The PTO designers at Rockford expected resistance and were prepared to respond.

At follow-up meetings, the two concerns were addressed. Rockford made some design modifications because sensitivity to employee issues was a core value. Rockford was going to discontinue sick-time payout upon termination for new employees. However, after thinking about workers' concerns, Rockford decided to freeze current workers' unused sick-time accounts and pay employees for sick time earned in excess of 480 hours. Swing people accepted this modification as fair and reasonable.

The conversion of Rockford's sick time payout (called Health-Rewards Program) to the new PTO program is based on the pro-rated formula in Figure 8-2.

When sick time is converted into cash, employees will be paid these percentages at their current base hourly rate. Employees who have up to 480 sick hours will retain hours to be used as CII, as outlined previously. (See Figure 8-3.)

Employees also had time to think about the reasons for change, and in particular, pressures on the hospital. Surprisingly, long-term workers who felt they had the most to lose with PTO eventually became the hospital's staunchest supporters. These long-term employees gave their all for the hospital and were also concerned about the hospital's welfare. With greater understanding of cost pressures on the hospital and Rockford's modification of the sick-time payout policy, the swing people and long-term employees became the strongest supporters of the conversion to PTO.

Figure 8-2
Conversion of Rockford's Sick Time Payout

Years of Service	Percentage of Cash Back of Hours > 480
5	25%
6	30%
7	35%
8	40%
9	45%
10	50%
11	52.5%
12	55%
13	57.5%
14	60%
15	62.5%
16	65%
17	67.5%
18	70%
19	72.5%
20	75%

Figure 8-3
Conversion Example

An employee has accrued the following paid time off under the pre-PTO system:

   a. 200 hours of vacation (25 days)

   b. 560 hours of sick time (70 days)

   c. 0 personal holidays

Under the PTO program, the employee will have:

   a. 200 hours in PTO Bank (former vacation time)

   b. 480 hours in CII Bank (former sick time)

   c. 80 hours paid at pro-rated percent of employee's hourly rate
      (based on above formula: 560 hours − 480 hours = 80 hours)

7. Implementation Companywide

Employee meetings were held to explain the program. Handouts were distributed. Swing people actually helped "sell" PTO throughout the hospital, and their support was important to obtaining buy-in from the workforce.

What follows is a summary of the comments of Rockford's HR officials: Heidi Elsbree, director of benefits, compensation and HRIS, and Dan Parod, vice president for human resources.

Elsbree views PTO as being beneficial for Rockford and employees. In particular, with PTO, employees are scheduling absences (vacation time) instead of using traditional sick time for single-day unscheduled absences. This is why the percent of unscheduled absences is so low. Also, managers are more willing to approve requests for partial-day absences (one to four hours) so that employees can schedule doctor visits, attend a child's school function or handle other nonwork issues without having to use a full day. In return, employees appreciate the greater flexibility and often work harder to fulfill daily work assignments, even though they work less than a full day.

In 2001, Rockford opened a daycare for children with a minor illness or injury (e.g., ear infections, sore throats, colds and skin infections) called TLC Sick Bay. Professional nurses staff the center from 6 a.m. to 9 p.m.Monday through Friday. Employees can pay for the care through payroll deductions. TLC Sick Bay accepts children from six weeks to 17 years old. Children with highly contagious illnesses such as chicken pox, measles and mumps are not accepted. Rockford also runs an on-site summer day camp for employees' children.

These programs further highlight Rockford's commitment to being an employer of choice and its desire to help employees with family and personal issues. The staff appreciate using the hospital's facilities for their children. Rockford also benefits due to the increase in attendance by staff.

According to Elsbree, the good working relationship between staff and management reduces employees' need to call in sick when time off is needed. The result is a win-win outcome for employees and management. In Rockford's case, the customer—the patient—ultimately benefits.

Elsbree also stated that based on employee feedback, the hospital introduced a cash-out provision in the year 2000. Employees can cash out up to 40 hours provided they have a remaining balance of 80 hours. The cash-out payments occur in the first week of April and December (a good way to help pay for holiday shopping).

About 26 percent to 30 percent of the workers take advantage of the cash out, with about 86 percent cashing out the maximum allowed. Employees like the policy because they receive extra pay, although they do not necessarily like having to pay additional taxes. The fiscal office feels the cashout is cost justified, especially because it reduces replacement costs and fosters increased productivity from greater attendance.

Parod said he feels PTO helps with recruitment and retention. Many competitors have PTO plans, and applicants welcome the flexibility of using a bank of time regardless of the reason for the absence. In particular, being able to use traditional sick time as PTO or vacation is viewed very positively. Finally, PTO fits in with Rockford's culture. Rockford values its staff and prides itself in having adult-adult relationships between management and employees. Meeting employee needs is very important, according to Parod, and he credits Rockford's employees together with the medical staff for maintaining the hospital's reputation for excellent health-care services. Rockford Memorial Hospital's experience over 13 years clearly shows how PTO benefits employers and workers. Perhaps this is why companies in all industries are moving toward adopting PTO.

Rockford's PTO Employee Handbook
1. What is the Paid Time Off Program? (PTO)
PTO is Rockford's versatile and comprehensive approach to pay for time away from work.

The PTO program recognizes an employee's need to schedule time away from work. Instead of separating paid time for vacation, illness and personal reasons, PTO combines the number of days that employees may take away from work. This arrangement gives employees greater flexibility to use the time according to their individual and family needs.

You will accrue a "bank" of flexible PTO days from which you can manage your paid time away from work.

You will also accrue Catastrophic Illness Insurance (CII) to provide income protection in the event of an extended illness or injury. CII will supply continuation of income to the extent that you have accrued time available.

2. Why was a new benefits program needed regarding paid time away from work?
Flexibility: Many employees have expressed concerns that the existing policies regarding paid time away from work were not meeting their individual or family needs. The PTO program is versatile enough to allow you to make the decisions when it comes to your time off. It reflects the corporate culture that has been

adopted at Rockford Memorial Hospital to give its employees maximum flexibility. **Recruitment:** Several health facilities (many are our competitors) within the Midwest are offing PTO programs. National surveys have found that among nurses, improving "time-off scheduling" was a top priority to complement recruitment incentives.

Retention: Nationally, more than 53 percent of respondents felt time-off scheduling was the top incentive/program for retention of nurses and health-care personnel.

3. What specific types of absences from work does PTO apply?

You can use PTO days for scheduled time off such as vacations or days you need off for personal reasons.

PTO also enables you to take time off for unscheduled personal and family matters that cause you to take time away from work. To be paid time off in the event of an unscheduled absence you must comply with hospital and departmental policies for notification of your absence.

Time off for bereavement, recognized holidays, jury service and military reserve does not come from PTO bank. Payment for these days away from work continues as under current policies.

4. Who is eligible for PTO program?

You are eligible for the PTO program if you are a regularly scheduled full-time employee (80 hours per pay period) or a regularly scheduled part-time employee (32 hours per pay period). You are not eligible if you work less than 32 hours per pay period or are a restricted part-time employee.

5. How do I accrue time in my PTO Bank?

Paid time away from work accrues per pay period in the bank based on years of service. The accrual rates are shown below:

Full-Time Accrual Rates			
Years of Service	Hrs./Pay Period	Hrs/Year	Days/Year
0 – 4	5.538	144	18
5 – 9	7.077	184	23
10+	8.615	224	28

Rockford Memorial Hospital recognizes the vital importance of its part-time employees and pro-rates paid time off based on employee's hours worked. These accrual rates are as follows:

Part-Time Accrual Rates

Years of Service	Hours/Hours Worked
0 – 4	0.069
5 – 9	0.088
10+	0.108

6. How much time can I accrue in my PTO Bank?

You will be allowed to accrue up to a maximum of 150 percent of your annual PTO accrual rate. The maximum number of hours allowable in the bank will not exceed 150 percent of the annual accrual amount. To enforce this maximum, managers will be notified on a quarterly basis if any of their employees are nearing the maximum.

The bank maximums are listed below:

Years of Service	Bank Maximum
0 – 4	27 days (216 hrs.)
5 – 9	35 days (280 hrs.)
10+	42 days (336 hrs.)

7. Example of Annual PTO Accrual:

Full-time employee
Accrual Rate: 18 days per year

Schedule of PTO days taken:

Year 1

PTO Time Taken		Summary Year 1	
2 weeks of vacation	10 days	Annual PTO days	18 days
Personal illness	3 days	Days taken	17 days
Personal time	4 days	Year–end Balance	1 PTO day
	17 PTO days		carried over to next year

Year 2 (begin year with 1 PTO day from prior year)

PTO Time Taken		Summary Year 2	
1 week of vacation	5 days	Beginning balance of PTO	1 Day
Personal illness	4 days	Annual PTO accrual	18 Days
Personal time	5 days	Total	19 Days
	14 PTO days	PTO days taken	–14 Days
		Year–end Balance	5 PTO days carried over to next year

Year 3 (begin year with 5 PTO days from prior year)

PTO Time Taken		Summary Year 3	
3 weeks of vacation	15 days	Beginning balance of PTO	5 days
Personal illness	4 days	Annual PTO accrual	18 days
Personal time	4 days	Total	23 days
	23 PTO	PTO days taken	23 days
		Year–end Balance	0 days

8. When do I begin to accrue time in PTO Bank?

You begin to accrue PTO as soon as you become an eligible employee. This would be upon your date of hire if you are a full-time or eligible part-time employee. If you are a noneligible existing employee of Rockford Memorial, you will begin to accrue PTO on the date you become eligible.

9. When can I start using my PTO days?

As a new employee, you must wait for a 90-day probationary period before you can start using your PTO benefits. If you are an existing Rockford Memorial employee and become eligible for PTO benefits, your 90-day probationary period will be waived.

10. When and how much paid time off should I schedule?

Rockford Memorial Hospital recognizes the value of paid time away from work. Therefore, the Hospital is confident employees and managers can work together to schedule time off in a way that continues Rockford Memorial's ability to serve our customers—our patients.

11. How do I accrue Catastrophic Illness Insurance (CII)?

Catastrophic Illness Insurance will provide continuation of income to employees in the event of a catastrophic illness or injury. Your coverage will begin on the eighth consecutive calendar day of illness or injury. Accrual will be by pay period to a maximum of seven days a year. The accrual rates are as follows:

Accrual Rates

Full-Time Employees	2.15 Hrs./Pay Period
(80 Hrs./Pay Period)	(56 Hrs./Year = 7 Days)
Part-Time Employees	0.027 Hrs./Hr. Worked
(32+ Hrs./Pay Period)	

12. How much time can I accrue in CII?

You may accumulate up to 480 hours in Catastrophic Illness Insurance. This is equal to 60 days (60 days x 8 hours per day = 480 hours). When you reach 480 hours, your accrual will stop and not resume until your bank is once again below the maximum. If you are still not working after 480 hours and you are eligible, your long-term disability insurance will start to take effect.

13. May I transfer PTO days into Catastrophic Illness Insurance?

No. Rockford Memorial Hospital recognizes the value of taking time away from work. Employees need time for rest, relaxation, and any other personal and family needs. These needs are the true purpose of the PTO program and the paid time away from work offered by the program are incorporated into the hospital's benefit package specifically for these needs.

Catastrophic Illness Insurance is designed to reflect seniority by the amount of coverage provided. In other words, the longer you have worked at Rockford Memorial Hospital, the more insurance you have earned. Therefore, Rockford Memorial Hospital is encouraging employees to use their PTO days for their individual and family needs, rather than sacrificing those needs now and accruing additional time in CII, which can only be accessed in the event of an extended illness or injury.

14. What happens to my accruals under the PTO program when I leave?

Your accrued PTO days as of your final day of employment at the Hospital will be paid to you at 100 percent of your current base hourly rate. Hours accrued in your CII account are not paid at termination.

15. How will Rockford Memorial convert from the existing program to the new PTO program?

The current program: Under the existing program, vacations are based on length of service. Full-time employees accumulate "sick" days at 12 per year and are given three "personal" days per year. Under the existing program, personal days **do not** accumulate and must be used in the year awarded. For full-time employees, vacation time corresponds to length of service as follows:

1 – 4 years of service	2 weeks (10 days)
5 – 9 years of service	3 weeks (15 days)
10 or more years of service	4 weeks (20 days)

Vacation for regular part-time employees is pro-rated based on the cumulative regular hours paid during the previous eligibility period.

Under the present Health Rewards System, sick time can accrue to a maximum of 1,300 hours and employees with greater than 480 hours in their sick bank are eligible for Health Rewards. Currently, employees are allowed to receive cash back at termination for all hours in excess of 480 based on the following formula:

Years of Service	% of Cash Back of Hours > 480
Less than 10	25%
10 – 20	50%
> 20	75%

Conversion to the new PTO program:

1. What happens to my accrued vacation time?

The vacation time that you have accrued will be transferred into your PTO bank on a 1 hour to 1 hour basis. In other words, 1 vacation day that you have now will become 1 PTO day in your bank.

2. What happens to my accrued sick time?

The conversion of our current Health-Rewards Program to the new PTO program allows employees to cash in their accumulated sick time more than 480 hours based on the pro-rated version of the formula shown under the Health Rewards System. This pro-rated version is as follows:

Years of Service	Percentage of Cash Back of Hours > 480)
5	25%
6	30%
7	35%
8	40%
9	45%
10	50%
11	52.5%
12	55%
13	57.5%
14	60%
15	62.5%
16	65%
17	67.5%
18	70%
19	72.5%
20	75%

When sick time is converted into cash, employees will be paid these percentages at their current base hourly rate. Employees who have up to 480 sick hours will retain hours to be used as catastrophic illness insurance as outlines previously.

16. Conversion Example 1
An employee has accrued:

64 hours of vacation	(8 days)
240 hours of sick time	(30 days)
8 hours of personal time	(1 day)

Upon Conversion to PTO program, the employee will now have:

64 hours of vacation time will become 64 hours of PTO time

240 hours of sick time will become 240 hours of CII time

The eight hours of personal time will not transfer over into the PTO Bank or into the CII Bank. Employee must use the time before PTO conversion date; otherwise it will be forfeited.

17. Conversion Example 2
An employee has accrued:

200 hours of vacation time	(25 days)
560 hours of sick time	(70 days)
0 personal time	

Upon Conversion to PTO program, the employee will now have:

200 hours of vacation time will become 200 hours of PTO time

560 hours of sick time will become 480 hours of CII time; and

80 hours paid will be paid to the employee at pro-rated percentage of employee's salary based on formula explained in No. 15 (560 sick hours – 480 = 80 hours)

Conclusion 9

PTO has come a long way since the early 1970s. Back then, hospitals (being a 24/7 operation) believed PTO would give their predominately female workforce (many of whom had family responsibilities) greater flexibility to meet personal and family obligations. As an additional benefit, hospitals reported PTO reduced unscheduled absences. This occurred by:

1. Giving employees greater ability and responsibility to self-manage their paid time off wisely
2. Emphasizing value for employees to schedule time off
3. Allowing managers to be more flexible in accommodating requests for paid absences, even if a request is for a few hours.

As a result, the increase in "presenteeism" increased productivity and reduced costs. For hospitals, this translated into greater continuity of care, which is very important for good patient care, and into a reduction of sick and replacement costs, which lowers overall costs.

Today, all industries (including health care) are confronted with high benefit costs that need to be controlled and employees asking for flexibility to help them balance work and nonwork pressures. This is why companies in all industries are adopting PTO designs. Of particular importance is the fact that employee support of PTO plans tend to increase over time. Many workers, who were somewhat suspicious at first, find PTO provides desired scheduling flexibility. They appreciate the greater sensitivity of managers in accommodating employee requests for paid time off, even in increments of a few hours, and understand the need for workers to give managers as much advance notice as possible when time off is important.

Surprisingly, the costs of pay for time not worked benefits can equal what companies pay for health care. A 2005 Mercer study found the cost of employer-provided health care in 2004 averaged the same percentage (14 percent) as the costs of traditional sick, vacation and holidays together with disability coverage (short-term and long-term disability and workers' compensation). In addition, to attract and retain workers, companies need to give employees greater flexibility so they can meet personal and family obligations. A 2006 SHRM study further reinforces the value of "creating a work environment that empowers employees to make decisions that affect the quality of their work life." *(Keeping Employees Engaged: A Strategic Factor in Motivation, Performance and Retention)*. PTO definitely meets this standard.

PTO has proven beneficial in the health-care industry, and research has shown PTO also fosters greater productivity and is seen as an employee morale booster for companies in all industries. The results of PTO are important for all companies as well, especially with cost pressures from global competition and the constant competition for talent.

Appendices

Example A:
Converting to a PTO System

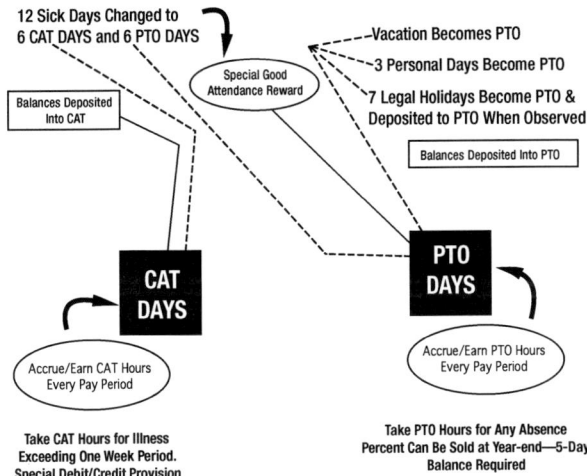

Figure A is an example of a company handout that describes pre-PTO and PTO systems. What might initially be seen as complicated and confusing becomes clearer as the speaker describes each activity. The handout lends itself to a PowerPoint presentation with each section being layered to help explain the PTO plan.

The handout shows employees the following:

A. **Top right hand section of chart**
   1. Pre-PTO vacation, personal days and legal holidays will now be called PTO days.
   2. Any pre-PTO balances of unused, earned vacation, personal days and legal holidays will be deposited into PTO upon conversion.

B. **Bottom right hand section of chart**
   1. PTO hours can be used for any absence. Employees will no longer need to tell their managers why time off is necessary.
   2. PTO time will accrue bi-weekly.
   3. PTO hours can be sold for cash at year end. A balance of five days must remain after cash in.

C. **Top left hand section of chart**
   1. Pre-PTO sick time will now accrue per pay period: six days in CAT and six days in PTO. Caps for each account will be explained.

2. Sick-time balances will be deposited into CAT upon conversion

3. Explanation of Special Good Attendance Reward highlights the way employees with good attendance can have unused, earned sick time deposited into PTO.

D. Bottom left hand section of chart

1. CAT hours are used for illnesses exceeding one week. Special Debit/Credit provision is explained, highlighting how a PTO account could be credited with CAT hours for first five days of absence due to personal illness.

2. CAT hours will accrue bi-weekly.

Example B:

Sample Company PTO Policy and Procedure

Policy Statement

The ABC Company recognizes the importance of providing employees with paid time off from work. The Paid Time Off (PTO) policy provides such time as a reward for service, and to provide employees with the opportunity for relaxation, to attend to personal responsibilities and to take time off for illness.

Procedures

1. Eligibility Requirements

All full-time employees (scheduled to work 80 hours per pay period) or part-time employees (scheduled to work at least 32 hours per pay period) are eligible to participate in the PTO program.

2. PTO Accounts

a. Employees will accrue time off into two accounts:

    1. Paid Time Off (PTO) account

    2. Catastrophic (CAT) account.

b. The PTO account is used for time off that historically has been used for sick, vacation and personal holidays.

c. The CAT account is used for longer-term personal illnesses. CAT time is used after an employee is absent from work because of a personal illness for four consecutive work days. The first four days of absence are paid from the PTO account. A physician's note is required to verify the illness and projected date of return to work.

d. Time off with pay for other days, for example, funeral leave, jury duty, military leave and legal holidays, continues as under current policies.

3. Annual Accruals of PTO and CAT Days/Hours

a. Full-time employees receive PTO days while in paid status based on the following current vacation schedules (A – C).

Full-Time Employees

Vacation Schedule/ Annual Days of Vacation	PTO Days/Hours *	PTO Hours Earned per Pay Period	CAT Hours Earned per Pay Period
A. 10 Days	18 (144)	5.540	2.4516
B. 15 days	23 (184)	7.080	2.4516
C. 20 days	28 (240)	8.616	2.4516

* PTO days include: annual vacation schedule, four personal days and four sick days

b. For example, a full-time employee under Vacation Schedule A will receive 5.54 hours of PTO time for every pay period while in paid status. At the end of the year, an employee will have earned 144 hours or 18 PTO days (5.54 hours x 26 pay periods = 144 PTO hours).

c. Full-time employees will earn 2.4615 CAT hours per pay period (based on working 80 hours per bi-weekly pay period). At the end of the year, an employee will have earned 64 hours or six CAT Days.

d. Employees hired under Vacation Schedule A will advance to Vacation Schedule B after six years of full-time employment (a total of 12,480 hours of employment). Employees will then advance to Vacation Schedule C after six more years of full-time employment (total of 24,960 hours of employment).

e. Increased PTO accruals will begin in the first pay period following completion of 12,480 hours or 24,960 hours of employment.

f. Employees hired under Vacation Schedule B will advance to Vacation Schedule C after six years of full-time employment (total of 12,480 hours of employment).

Part-Time Employees

a. Part-time employees earn PTO time according to actual hours worked, based on a maximum of 80 hours worked in a bi-weekly pay period. The following chart identifies the number of PTO days. Actual hours are based on hours worked.

Vacation Schedule Annual Days of Vacation	PTO Days *	Accrual Rate for Hours Worked	CAT Hours Earned per Hours Worked
A. 10 Days	14	.0539	.0308
B. 15 Days	19	.0731	.0308
C. 20 Days	24	.0924	.0308

* PTO Days include vacation time and four sick days.

b. For example, a part-time employee (Vacation Schedule A) works 32 hours per pay period. The employee will earn 44.8 PTO hours by the end of the 26th pay period (one year of employment). 32 hours x 26 pay period = 832 hours x .0539 = 44.8 PTO hours

c. If the same employee worked with Vacation Schedule B, the employee would have earned 60.8 PTO hours by the end of 26 pay periods. 32 hours x 26 pay periods = 832 hours x .0731 = 60.8 PTO hours

d. Part-time employees accrue CAT time based on hours worked per year. The accrual rate is .0308 hours per scheduled work hour. For example, if a part-time employee worked 32 hours per pay period, the employee would earn 25.6 CAT hours by the end of 26 pay periods. 32 hours x 26 pay periods = 832 hours x .0308 = 25.6 PTO hours

4. **Annual Maximums/Caps for PTO and CAT Accounts**

   a. For full-time employees, the maximum accruals are:

   For PTO = 150 percent of the annual allowance. For example, if the annual PTO allowance is 18 days (144 hours), the 150 percent cap is 27 days (216 hours). For CAT = 70 days (856 hours)

   b. For part-time employees, the maximum accruals are:

   For PTO = 150 percent of annual PTO allowance.

   For CAT = 47 days (376 hours).

5. **When Do Employees Earn PTO and CAT Time?**

New employees begin to earn PTO and CAT time on their date of hire.

6. **When Can Employees Use PTO and CAT Time?**

   a. Employees can use PTO and CAT time after completion of the 60-day probationary period. During probation, employees accrue PTO and CAT time but cannot use it until they pass probation.

   b. Only earned PTO and CAT time can be used. Advancement of time is not permitted.

   c. An employee who becomes ill while on the job and cannot continue to work the full shift will be paid for time worked and then use PTO time to pay for balance of the work day.

   d. PTO hours will be considered as time worked for purposes of calculating overtime. CAT hours paid will not be considered as time worked for purposes of calculating overtime.

7. **Cash Conversion of PTO Time**

   a. Employees can trade in up to four PTO days per year at 100 percent of their value. The cash-out amounts are subject to applicable taxes.

   b. The cash-out option can be used every November and May.

   c. Employees must have a balance of five PTO days after cash out.

8. **Family and Medical Leave Act (FMLA)**

   a. For personal illnesses covered under FMLA, an employee can use PTO time for the first four work days of an absence. Beginning with the fifth consecutive work day absent due to personal illness, an employee can use CAT time for the balance of the absence. Employees are required to have their personal physicians complete necessary FMLA forms.

   b. For intermittent absences due to personal illness, an employee will use PTO time for the first four days (32 hours) of absence. Beginning with the fifth day, CAT time can be used. Employees are required to have their personal physicians complete necessary FMLA forms.

c. For other FMLA absences (e.g., to care for an immediate family member), an employee can only use PTO time.

9. Workers' Compensation

Employees will be paid from the CAT account for the waiting period of seven calendar days (five work days). If the employee does not have sufficient CAT time, the PTO account can be used.

10. Long-Term Disability

An employee will use PTO hours for the first four days of absence, if available. Thereafter, the employee will be paid CAT time, if available. Upon using all CAT hours, the employee would use the remaining PTO time until the long-term disability waiting period is over.

11. Payment of PTO and CAT Upon Termination

a. Employees who terminate with sufficient notice will receive payment for all unused, earned PTO time. CAT time will not be paid out.

b. An employee discharged for cause will forfeit any PTO time.

c. If an employee dies while having a PTO balance, the employee's estate will receive payment for the balance of PTO time. CAT time will not be paid out.

d. An employee who terminates and then is rehired within two months will be credited with the previous CAT amount as of the termination date. Employees rehired after two months will not receive credit for the previous CAT balance.

12. Impact of PTO Accruals Due to Change of Status

a. Employees who change from full-time to part-time status may either (1) use the balance of PTO time before commencing part-time status, or (2) receive payment for 50 percent of the PTO balance as of the date part-time status begins and then carry over the other 50 percent in their PTO account.

b. The balance of the CAT hours will be credited up to the maximum for part-time status.

13. PTO and CAT Pay for Shift Work

a. Employees assigned to work permanent evening or night shifts will be paid PTO and CAT time at their evening/night shift rates.

b. Employees who rotate between day and evening/night shifts will be paid PTO and CAT time at their day-shift rate.

14. PTO and Legal Holiday Time

If an employee is scheduled to work on an observed legal holiday, the employee will receive the work day hours in the PTO account for use in the future.

15. Conversion Policy

At the time of conversion to PTO, employees who have balances of unused, earned vacation, sick or personal holidays will have time credited in the following way:

a. Time Deposited into PTO Account
    - Unused, earned vacation and personal holiday time
    - Up to 24 hours of earned, unused sick time

b. Time Deposited into CAT Account
    - Balance of unused, earned sick time in excess of 24 hours

For example, an employee at conversion has a balance of:
    - 70 hours of vacation time
    - 50 hours of sick time
    - 8 hours of personal time

The employee's **PTO** account will be credited with **102 hours** (70 hours of vacation; 8 hours of personal time; and 24 hours of sick time).

The employee's **CAT** account will be credited with **26 hours** of sick time (50 hours – 24 hours).

Employees with more than 100 percent of the annual vacation allotment will be paid for hours in excess of 100 percent of the allotment at 100 percent value. The remaining 100 percent vacation allotment will be credited to the employee's PTO account.

For example, an employee's annual pre-PTO vacation allotment is 80 hours. However, the employee has 110 unused, earned vacation hours. Upon conversion to PTO, the employee will be paid 30 hours at the employee's hourly rate (110 hours – 80 hours = 30 hours). The remaining 80 hours will be credited to the employee's PTO account.

PTO and CAT accumulation caps will go into effect after one year of PTO.

Example C:
Employee PTO Handbook—Q&A Format

When explaining the PTO plan in a handbook for workers, we found it is best to use a question-and-answer format. We ask swing people to help us identify questions (to ensure we are asking all the right questions) and review answers to ensure clarity. Modifications are made based on swing people's comments.

The following is a table of contents from a company's Employee PTO Information Handbook.

1. What is the paid time off (PTO) program?
2. Why is the company implementing PTO?
3. What specific types of absences from work does PTO apply?
4. Who is eligible for the PTO program?
5. How do I accrue time in my PTO bank?
6. How much time can I accrue in my PTO bank?
7. Examples of PTO accruals
8. When do I begin to accrue time in my PTO Bank?
9. When can I start using my PTO days?
10. When and how much PTO can I schedule at one time?
11. How do I accrue time in the catastrophic account (CAT)?
12. How much time can I accrue in CAT?
13. Can I trade-in any PTO time and receive cash for the days?
14. What happens to my accruals under PTO when I leave?
15. How will the company convert unused, earned pre-PTO time into PTO program?
16. Will I lose any time upon conversion?

Example D:

Sample Employee Handout Explaining PTO

1. Why is the company converting to a Paid Time Off (PTO) system?

A PTO system offers employees flexibility to deal with work and nonwork demands. In the past, the company had a time-off system that pried into employees' personal lives, because they were asked why they needed time off. A PTO system recognizes employees have needs for time off, and management does not need to know specific reasons (unless required by law). All time off is placed into two buckets of time—a paid time off bank (PTO) called a PTO account and a catastrophic (CAT) account.

2. How does the PTO system work?

The PTO system gives employees the choice between taking a day off for pay or selling the day back for extra pay.

To employees, a day off with pay—for vacation, personal, holiday, illness or legal holiday—is a paid day off. With the PTO system, the company places all this time into one bucket called a PTO bank.

Every December, employees may trade in unused, earned PTO time for cash (100 percent value). The employee must have a balance of eight PTO days after trade in.

Currently, employees receive 12 sick days per year. With the PTO system, six sick days are placed in the PTO bank, and the remaining six sick days are placed in the CAT account. CAT hours are used for illnesses when an employee is out of work for more than five consecutive work days.

The employee is paid from the PTO bank for the first five consecutive work days of absence due to personal illness. Time in excess of five days is paid from the CAT account.

3. How much PTO and CAT time will I receive?

PTO is measured by days, because the definition of a work day varies. PTO applies to full-time employees whether or not they are scheduled to work eight hours per day (40 hours per week) or 7.5 hours per day (37.5 hours per week).

Currently, full-time employees receive vacation time, three personal days, seven legal holidays and 12 sick days per year. The total amount of paid time off available varies according to years of service. The following table illustrates current annual paid time off benefits.

Years of Service	0 – 4	4 – 10	10 – 20	20 – 30	30 +
Vacation Days	10	15	20	25	30
Personal Days	3	3	3	3	3
Legal Holidays	7	7	7	7	7
Sick Days	12	12	12	12	12
Total Days Off	32	37	42	47	52

With PTO, employees will keep their current annual vacation time, personal days and legal holidays. In addition, of the 12 sick days previously provided, six sick days will be added to the PTO account. The remaining six sick days will be added to the CAT account.

Total Annual PTO/CAT Days

Years of Service	0 – 4	4 – 10	10 – 20	20 – 30	30 +
Total PTO Days	26	31	36	41	46
Total CAT Days	6	6	6	6	6
Total Days	32	37	42	47	52

Note that the total annual amount of paid time off using PTO/CAT is the same as the time provided in the pre-PTO systems.

4. **What will happen to my personal days, vacation time and sick leave when the company converts to PTO system?**

   a. All unused, earned vacation time and personal days will be added to your PTO account.

   b. All unused, earned sick time will be added to the CAT account.

5. **What paid time will I use if I am sick shortly after the conversion to PTO?**
In theory, the time should be charged to the PTO account. However, the company realizes that many workers will have balances of sick time in their pre-PTO accounts. Therefore, in fairness to employees with sick-time balances, the company is providing a one-time swap of sick time for PTO upon conversion based on the following chart. In this way, employees who need sick time after PTO conversion will be able to use some pre-PTO sick time. After the swap, the remaining sick time will be added to the CAT accounts.

Hours in Sick Leave Account At the Time of Conversion to PTO	Days Allowed to be Swapped for PTO
< 8	0
8 – 24	1
25 – 48	2
49 – 96	3
97 – 160	4
161 – 240	5
241 +	6

For example, an employee with 97 hours (12 days) in a pre-PTO sick leave account at the time of conversion will have four days added to PTO account.

6. **Suppose I have a heart attack; am I expected to use my PTO time because I am sick?**

No. The idea behind PTO is to use PTO days for intermittent or illnesses of short durations. Remember that six PTO days were previously sick days. When an illness exceeds five consecutive work days, an employee qualifies to use the CAT account hours.

7. **Is there ever a time when an employee does not have to use PTO for an illness?**

Yes. If an employee is hospitalized overnight during the catastrophic illness, upon return to work, the employee can request up to five of the remaining CAT days be transferred to PTO for waiting period reimbursement.

8. **What if I am absent due to an illness for more than five consecutive work days, return to work, and then have a relapse? Why should I have to use another five days of PTO time to satisfy a new waiting period?**

You might not have to use another five PTO days for the second waiting period. The company's policy is that if you return to work from an illness and have a relapse (attributed to the original illness) within 14 days of returning to work, you do not have to satisfy another waiting period before using CAT time.

9. **Do I use PTO or CAT time if I am on FMLA intermittent leave for a medical problem (e.g., chemotherapy or pregnancy complications)?**

If you have an FMLA-qualified need for intermittent leave that has been properly documented and approved by the HR department, you will be able to use CAT time. This is how it will work: The first five days will be paid from the PTO account. All further FMLA intermittent leave will be paid from CAT account.

For example, after the five-day waiting period is satisfied, treatment days will be paid from a CAT account.

10. **What happens to PTO and CAT time when I resign or retire?**

When you resign, you will be paid for all unused, earned PTO time. CAT time will not be paid out.

When you retire, unused, earned CAT time will be added to your years of service to enhance your monthly retirement benefit.

11. **How do I use PTO time?**

You should follow your department procedures for requesting time off. Some departments need longer advance notice for scheduling time off than others. PTO days belong to employees and the company wants workers to be able to use the time freely. The only requirement is that the remaining employees meet departmental needs while others are out on PTO.

Abbreviated Version as One-Page Summary

Vacation: renamed PTO and increases with tenure per current vacation schedule. Time accrues bi-weekly.

Personal Days: become PTO days. Time accrues bi-weekly

Legal Holidays are PTO days. Holiday time is posted to your PTO account in the pay period when holiday is observed. If you work the legal holiday, you have extra time in your PTO account to use in the future.

Sick days (12): Split. Six days accrue to PTO and six days accrue in CAT account.

CAT (catastrophic) account used for personal illnesses of more than five consecutive work days. If an employee is hospitalized overnight during a catastrophic illness, upon return to work the employee can request that up to five of any remaining CAT days be transferred to PTO for waiting period reimbursement.

PTO account max is equal to two times annual PTO allotment.

CAT account max is 70 days.

December PTO 100 percent buyback. Employee must have eight days remaining after pay out.

At Conversion to PTO:

- All unused, earned vacation, personal days added to PTO
- All unused, earned sick time added to CAT.

Special one-time swap

- One sick day for one PTO day based on following table
- Remaining days deposited in CAT.

Table for Swap

Balance of Sick Hours	PTO Days Added
< 8	0
8 – 24	1
25 – 48	2
49 – 96	3
97 – 160	4
161 – 240	5
240 +	6

Example E

Questions/Answers from WorldatWork Live Web Chat About PTO Issues

The following are 58 questions about PTO asked by HR professionals during a live Web chat. M. Michael Markowich provided the answers.

1. **Question:** To control absenteeism, do you feel there are benefits to having a centralized person to manage leave rather than having the control at the department level?
    Answer: Generally, absenteeism is managed at the department level. However, it is really up to the company to decide what is best. I prefer department control as long as the departmental managers understand the policies.

2. **Question:** What are the main advantages of PTO over traditional sick-leave plans?
    Answer: It is primarily psychological. PTO is the employee's time rather than the company's time to possibly be abused. PTO saves the company money by reducing the amount of traditional sick time granted in PTO accounts. The reduction results from employees having ownership of their time. Workers do not want to abuse their own time. This is what I mean by the main advantage of PTO is psychological.

3. **Question:** What is a typical implementation time frame?
    Answer: You should plan for at least six months. The bulk of the time is used to communicate with employees. Also, top management may raise questions that will require additional fiscal analysis.

4. **Question:** My company plans to implement a PTO program in the very near future. Is there a recommended method of transition? What are the pitfalls and how to avoid them?
    Answer: First, do a thorough fiscal review. It is critical that top management and HR clearly understand the costs of the current attendance system. In this way, you will receive greater support for any change. Also, involve employees and managers in task forces to help you finalize the design. People help support what they create. Therefore, involvement will greatly enhance employee acceptance. Finally, be prepared to share with employees the benefits to the company and workers to control unscheduled absence costs.

5. **Question:** What are innovative ways to encourage staff to report PTO taken if your policy is "use it or lose it"?

Answer: I recommend that PTO not have a "use it or lose it" clause. Employees should be encouraged to take time, but not to have a zero balance by a certain date. Part of the problem with traditional attendance programs is the "use it or lose it" concept. It encourages abuse because no one wants to lose a benefit.

6. **Question:** We are considering implementing a PTO program. Because employees would accrue PTO time, we are wondering if we should advance new hires a few days of PTO.

   Answer: I am opposed to advancing time for new hires. Think about this. You work and then get paid—rather than get paid and then work. Therefore, why grant time off before it is earned?

7. **Question:** We are in an industry that has plants, warehouses, sales offices and a main headquarters building. The plant and warehouse workers are classified as hourly nonexempt, and they do not earn sick pay. Generally, the office workers and all professional employees are salaried and do receive sick pay, along with a higher level of short-term disability. Some of our clerical workers in plants are hourly (no sick pay) and some are salaried. We are looking at consistency and deciding in which direction to go for office workers in plants. What is your experience with this type of situation and do you have any recommendations?

   Answer: It seems your company needs to decide if all employees should receive sick time. Based on your decision, I suggest that you then consider PTO for workers who are eligible for sick time. On a personal note, I encourage employers to grant sick time to all workers regardless of their position. We are all human, and sick-time payments (if managed well) are well appreciated and good for morale.

8. **Question:** From experience, what were the key elements of successful conversions of a traditional time away program with separate sick and vacation accounts to PTO?

   Answer: Key elements include a communication strategy that enables employees to clearly understand the costs of traditional paid time off programs and the value to both employees and the employer of controlling absenteeism. Also, involving a task force of workers to work with HR to finalize PTO design is helpful. Employee involvement helps to "sell" PTO to workers.

9. **Question:** Our PTO plan is divided into categories. We use planned and unplanned time off. Our concern is that if we put them all in one category,

employees will not plan their time appropriately, and we will have several unexpected absences. Is this a legitimate concern?

Answer: I feel you are causing yourself additional administrative work. The value of PTO is it is the employee's time. Therefore, I would not place time off as planned and unplanned. It seems you are concerned with unplanned absences. You may want to consider a no-fault absentee control approach to manage excessive unplanned absences.

10. **Question:** Is it reasonable to track scheduled versus unscheduled days or are you then defeating the main purpose of PTO?

    Answer: Ideally, you should be able to track scheduled versus unscheduled absences. This does not defeat the main premise of PTO. The tracking helps to discipline for excessive absences. PTO does not eliminate unscheduled absences. Also, the tracking helps to quantify the impact of PTO.

11. **Question:** Do companies employ a third party to monitor time off? If so, is there a period of time off before the third-party administrator is to be contacted?

    Answer: Companies self-manage PTO programs. It is really no different than self-managing traditional sick, vacation or personal time accounts.

12. **Question:** Are there any general guidelines about handling reserved balances in excess of the prescribed accrual hours?

    Answer: I do not recommend allowing employees to accrue time in excess of the PTO maximum. Employees need time away from work. A cap is necessary, because unused time becomes more expensive with salary increases. This is why PTO time is provided with maximum levels of accruals. Some companies have unlimited CAT time because CAT is not paid out at the time of resignation.

13. **Question:** If one is transitioning from a traditional paid time off program to PTO, how does one "convert" the accumulated time of long-service employees? Is there a cost that needs to be recognized up front?

    Answer: PTO accumulates time with a cap (e.g., 150 percent) of the annual allotment. Often, current company practices enable workers to have more than the 150 percent cap. You should consider the following options:

    a. If the cash is available, pay down workers to a number below the cap (e.g., 100 percent of the annual PTO allotment).

    b. Freeze accounts until employees use time and begin accruals after workers fall below cap.

    c. Give workers one or two years to take time off so that employees have used sufficient time to be below caps by the beginning of the second or third year of PTO.

14. **Question:** How do you draw the line between allowing some "unplanned absences" and making clear to employees that too many absences is grounds for disciplinary action?

    Answer: Your point illustrates why I recommend a no-fault absentee control program. No-fault defines what is excessive and identifies consequences.

15. **Question:** Are there positive methods that can be used to reward employees for perfect attendance? Are there different programs for salaried versus hourly employees?

    Answer: Many companies have implemented traditional reward programs to motivate employees to be good attendees. In reality, these reward programs end up rewarding the wrong workers. Good attendees will have good attendance records regardless of the reward system. It is in their blood to come to work. In contrast, abusers value time off with pay—when they want to take time off. Reward programs will not cause abusers to change their behavior. The only intervention I know that works for abusers is the no-fault absentee control program.

16. **Question:** This is my first experience with a company with a class of employees who receive no sick pay. Is this common in the manufacturing industry?

    Answer: Many manufacturing companies offer no sick pay. You need to think about what benefits you need to attract and retain workers. I had a client that offered no sick pay. I was contacted because they had a sick-time problem. Workers at this company valued time off—when they wanted it—even if they were not paid. The unscheduled absences caused production problems. The shop manager never knew how many workers would show up. We implemented a PTO program that included some time off for illnesses. Unscheduled absences decreased.

17. **Question:** How do you move from traditional vacation, sick pay, short-term disability and other policies to a PTO policy without alienating employees?

    Answer: Your communication strategy should highlight why it is in the employees' best interest as well as the company's to convert to PTO. Also, I suggest using an employee task force to assist management in the design of PTO. The task force can be used as a "test market" for PTO design. Employee feedback will help you gauge employee reactions and enable you to modify the plan if necessary.

    There will be resistance to PTO. You are implementing it to save money.

The key is not to avoid upset, but to manage it.

18. **Question:** Would seniority be the key factor for accrual rate differences?

    Answer: Yes, to the extent seniority affects current vacation accruals.

19. **Question:** What are your opinions regarding what hours PTO accrues on (for example, regular worked hours, excused absences due to low workloads, maximum number of hours worked in a pay period, hours for which PTO is being used, etc.)? In other words, on what recorded hours should PTO not accrue?

    Answer: What are your current practices? Most companies accrue based on scheduled hours worked, although some of my clients used actual hours worked (excluding overtime). It is really up to your company. That is why I asked about your current practices. Most companies account PTO time based on current practices so that there is one less reason for change to explain to employees.

20. **Question:** What are your thoughts about allowing employees to donate time for co-workers to use in hardship situations?

    Answer: Companies that enable workers to donate time for other workers to use in hardship situations usually have a culture that supports this type of giving. Clearly, there are benefits, especially to workers who have hardships. However, you need to consider cost implications and what happens if a worker who donated time now needs time and there is no time available.

21. **Question:** For companies switching from traditional sick and vacation leave accumulation plans to PTO, which of the following has worked better?

    a. Mandatory conversion and participation

    b. Option to stay under old plan

    c. Convert to new one.

    If offered an option, how long is best to run the dual system?

    Answer: I would recommend that you convert all workers to PTO. Running a dual system can end up being an administrative nightmare. Multifacility companies often stagger implementation due to logistics.

22. **Question:** Is there a recommended method for handling accrued sick/vacation time above established maximums?

    Answer: You should not allow accruals to exceed maximums. If they do, companies either cashed-out time up to a maximum amount, strongly encouraged workers to take time off, or gave workers a period of time (12–18 months) to take time off so that balances would fall below the maximum. Thereafter, maximums will be enforced.

As difficult as this may sound, PTO time is granted "to be used." It is up to management to find ways for workers to get time off. If workers are unable to take time off, do not be surprised if they eventually take it—while being ill. We all need time off with pay.

23. **Question:** If it does not matter how PTO days are used, and they are no longer referred to as sick, vacation or personal days, how can you effectively incorporate a corrective action policy for abuse of time off (unscheduled versus scheduled absences)? Do you have any examples of the parameters of a no-fault absentee control program?

    Answer: You need to be able to document whether the absence was scheduled or not. PTO speaks to how an employee is to be paid, not how an employee is to be disciplined. For more information about no-fault absentee control programs, I suggest reading the WorldatWork building block, *Paying and Managing Absences*.

24. **Question:** Should an employer be concerned about financial risk in allowing employees to transfer time to co-workers—in that if paid out according to receiving employee's hourly rate, the pay may be higher than that of the employee who extends the gift.

    Answer: Yes, and an employee needs to think about future needs before donating time.

25. **Question:** Referring to my earlier question about PTO donations to another employee—this would not go into a bank and have a third-party committee determine who gets how much. This would be employee A signing a form to transfer x hours to employee B. Employee A would decide to whom to give it and how many hours employee B would receive. This is much more in keeping with our culture. Your comments please.

    Answer: I may have some misgivings that I previously mentioned about your practice. However, if your practice dovetails with your culture, keep it going.

26. **Question:** Are there any attendance incentive plans being designed that allow employees to accumulate unlimited sick time and sell their sick leave back to the company upon retirement (similar to some teacher retirement programs), or are there perfect attendance awards (financial) that are being offered by companies?

    Answer: Accumulating unlimited sick time and selling it at retirement at one time was cost-effective. Today it is cost prohibitive. This is why companies that had such a program are converting to PTO as a way to discontinue the practice.

27. **Question:** In an effort to recognize the changing needs of today's workforce, leave programs are being developed to include domestic partner benefits. As a soft benefit, employees are often extended the leave opportunity to care for an ill domestic partner or a child from the household of that partner. Leave programs for a death in the family are also being extended to domestic partners. Based on your experience, what issues if any, are associated with allowing this, and what is the typical cost associated with extending this benefit to domestic partners and what are the trends?

    Answer: Nontraditional time-off practices are evolving. The key question is cost. Countering cost is a company culture supporting diversity and equality among all groups of workers.

28. **Question:** There are many benefits to implementing PTO. What are some of the pitfalls that a company could encounter?

    Answer: It takes considerable time and effort to design and communicate PTO so that all employees thoroughly understand it. Also, some employees will not like PTO. It is a change, and some workers may end up with less paid time off. Therefore, you can expect pockets of resistance. Not all companies believe employee upset is worth the potential savings.

29. **Question:** I wonder if one of the perceived negatives of PTO is for parents of young children who currently are high users of sick time to care for their children who are unable to go to school/day care. Are there effective solutions to such unique needs (other than bumping up the PTO allowance across the board)?

    Answer: PTO includes less sick time than was available under pre-PTO sick time accounts. Therefore, a company needs to believe that reducing unscheduled absences (for all reasons—not just child care) makes sense. In reality, high users of sick time may not like PTO. This is why a thorough fiscal analysis is recommended to cost-justify any conversion to PTO.

30. **Question:** Would you recommend PTO for a company that does not, in general, have an attendance problem?

    Answer: Yes, PTO could provide additional flexibility for employees when taking time off. PTO also helps workers better balance work and meeting personal and family obligations.

31. **Question:** What do you recommend as a waiting period before a new hire can use accrued PTO time?

    Answer: Common practice is three to six months, although some industries have a waiting period as long as 12 months (which I personally feel is too long).

32. **Question:** Employees sometimes prefer to take unpaid time off, even if they have balance of time in PTO account. What are your thoughts on this practice?

    Answer: Most companies require employees to take PTO time for any absence. The main reason is that time paid in the future may be more expensive due to wage increases.

33. **Question:** Do employees perceive PTO as a reduction of benefits?

    Answer: Employees who take the maximum number of sick days under the current system may feel PTO is a reduction or take-away. Good attendees usually favor PTO because they will be getting additional days off with pay.

34. **Question:** What are some of the successful practices with regard to providing incentives for employees to use their PTO time wisely?

    Answer: Under current sick-time practices, many employees perceive sick time as the company's—"if I don't use it, I will lose it." In contrast, with PTO, the time is the employee's. Therefore, why abuse your own time?

35. **Question:** Can you provide some of the most common (and successful) PTO provisions?

    Answer:

    a. Reasonable number of sick days packaged together with vacation and personal time

    b. Ability for employee to use minimum of 15 minutes for paid time off

    c. Willingness of managers to try to accommodate employee requests for time off

    d. High employee understanding of why the company moved to PTO and how PTO benefits employees and the company

    e. Involvement of an employee task force to help management with design and implementation of PTO

    g. Cash-out provision for workers to trade in some PTO time for cash.

36. **Question:** One of the things I have seen happen with PTO is employees coming to work when they are sick. Pretty soon a lot of people are sick, but they are reluctant to stay home because they would rather use PTO to do something fun, not stay home to recuperate. Any ideas about how to address this issue?

    Answer: You do not want "sick" employees at work. It is up to management to either refer employees to an on-site health nurse (if available) or if one is not available, to send "sick" employees home. Companies are required to provide a safe working environment. Having a sick person next to healthy employees can and will cause other workers to become ill. Allowing this to occur does not make good business or employee-relations sense. PTO includes time for illnesses. Why not use it if an employee is ill?

37. **Question:** Do you have a best-practices recommendation for a maternity policy? My company wants to offer additional paid benefits beyond what our state's temporary disability allows. Also, can you provide different benefits for maternity/paternity?

    Answer: I recommend that your maternity policy be included with your medical leave policy. At one time, companies had separate practices. Now the trend is to have just one medical policy for all medically related absences. In this way you are being consistent.

38. **Question:** How does it help to have a cap that prevents additional accrual once the maximum hours are accrued until time is used, especially if you have a manager or a work situation that prevents you from taking time off? In essence, it appears you "lose" time. Are there recommended alternatives?

    Answer: You are identifying a management problem that can be prevalent whether or not you have a PTO program or traditional paid time off practices. It is up to top management to ensure that workers are allowed to take time off. Some companies use HR to monitor company practices by auditing computer reports that analyze time-off utilization. HR can then interact with managers when workers come close to maximum to figure out ways for employees to take time off. Eventually, it is up to top executives to enforce time-off policies.

39. **Question:** What is the best way to integrate short-term disability plans with PTO plans?

    Answer: You can decide to allow employees to use PTO for the waiting period, or allow employees to use a pro-rated portion of PTO so the daily wage is 100 percent.

40. **Question:** At termination of employment, do most employers pay unused PTO at 100 percent?

    Answer: Yes. This is another advantage of PTO, because the time is the employees' to use (hopefully) wisely, instead of possibly abusing it. You should also consider a cap to control costs.

41. **Question:** How do most companies decide how many days to offer under a PTO program when converting from a traditional time off (sick/vacation/personal time) program?

Answer: First, determine the average annual use of sick days per employee (e.g., six days). Then decide how aggressively you want to control costs. If controlling costs is important, a company would place less than six days in the PTO account (e.g., four days). You need to balance cost savings against sensitivity to possible adverse employee relations, especially if you place less than the average use of sick days (six days in this example) in the PTO account.

42. **Question:** How do you convince top management that adding a few days to the vacation schedule as part of the transition to PTO (eliminating the separate sick-pay policy) will ultimately decrease the company's sick pay cost?

    Answer: Determine the cost of current absences; then use the review to cost-justify the number of PTO days. It does not matter how PTO days are used. They are no longer referred to as sick, vacation or personal days.

43. **Question:** How many companies allow PTO time to be carried over to the next year?

    Answer: Most designs offer a cap to replace the traditional "use or lose" concept. The cap allows employees to carry over unused, earned PTO to the next year. Just ask yourself this question: How would you feel if you lost time due to "use or lose" policy, especially if you felt your manager would not let you take time before you lost it?

44. **Question:** Please explain a no-fault approach to manage abuse.

    Answer: With "no-fault," the company decides the number of absences that will trigger disciplinary action. The reason for the absence is not considered, except for absences covered by laws (FMLA, ADA, workers' compensation, jury duty, military leave, etc.). Bereavement leaves are also not included. For more information, I suggest that you read "When is Excessive Absenteeism Grounds for Disciplinary Action," an online article at WorldatWork, or purchase the WorldatWork building block *Paying and Managing Absences*.

45. **Question:** Is it worthwhile to have a PTO policy in a manufacturing environment? Why?

    Answer: Yes. Manufacturing environments have the same problems as other industries do. Employees need time off with pay, and manufacturing workers have the same nonwork pressures causing them to call in sick as employees in other industries have. These factors affect recruitment and retention.

46. **Question:** Do you have suggestions about how to effectively communicate moving to a PTO with employees?

Answer: Use a task force of employees to help you communicate PTO. You need to be candid with workers and I recommend that you make the fiscal case about why PTO is in the employees' and company's best interest. The employee task force becomes your "test market."

47. **Question:** When PTO is accrued, do companies generally allow employees to "go in the hole"—carry a negative PTO balance?

    Answer: No. What happens if an employee leaves while owing the company money? It is not always easy to collect what is owed. Also, it is not a good idea to give employees an interest-free loan.

48. **Question:** Assuming a PTO plan is in place, what is standard practice when an employee reduces full-time employment, say from 100 percent to 50 percent, and the PTO accrued will exceed the maximum accrual level for the reduced full-time employee status?

    Answer: When an employee goes from full time to part time, the accruals are reduced. Companies have a maximum for part time just as they do for full time. If the balance is greater than when an employee is full time, companies can often do the following:

    a. Encourage employees to use paid time off before making the switch from full-time status to part time.

    b. Cash out a percentage of PTO time so that the PTO balance is below the maximum for part time.

    c. Permit the employee to work as part time, and give the worker one year to take time off so that the balance is below the maximum.

49. **Question:** What is the best way to measure the increases/decreases in costs for time off banks?

    Answer: Have a good starting number (prior to PTO) as your base. Then compare data for subsequent years against the base.

50. **Question:** I understand some companies credit an employee's CAT account for time in excess of the PTO maximum. What are your feelings about this practice?

    Answer: Some companies do this to show workers they are not losing time, even if they do not take PTO. However, the main concern is that workers need time off with pay. Providing a way for workers to continue working without breaks can result in health problems for the employees. Therefore, I recommend what many companies do—to monitor PTO use. Management should intervene and talk with managers about creative ways to schedule time off for workers, especially those near their PTO caps. The HR professional can be the staff person to monitor PTO use and talk with affected managers.

51. Question: What happens to an employee's PTO and CAT accounts if the worker dies while employed?

Answer: Companies often pay the PTO balance to the employee's estate. CAT time is not paid out.

52. Question: We are updating our policies, and exempt employees currently have more generous sick and vacation accruals than nonexempt employees. Is this a common practice among other employers? (We are in the financial industry.) Also, if we choose to make the policy equal for both groups, how do you suggest we implement the policy change?

Answer: Some companies elect to treat exempt and nonexempt personnel differently. However, the trend today is for all employees to receive the same sick and personal time, with vacation time varying by tenure and position.

53. Question: Our company has a formal PTO program with supporting HR policies. We require "exempt" staff to use PTO in hourly increments. It has always been my understanding that this practice jeopardizes the "exempt" status of an employee because treating their time in an hourly manner is inconsistent with the notion of being a salaried employee. Although I have come across documentation stating that this practice is OK as long as it is part of a formal PTO program, there appears to be court cases going "both ways." The most conservative approach is to use half- or full-day increments (versus hourly). What do you recommend?

Answer: Wage and Hour (a division of the Department of Labor) does not care how an exempt employee is paid (which accounts are charged or if the payroll system pays the worker in hours) as long as the exempt worker receives the projected salary. Where you could have problems is if you dock an exempt employee in hourly increments and consequently the salaried person is not paid a full salary. I suggest that you contact your local Wage and Hour Division for further guidance. Finally, I am not aware of any special status that PTO as a program has on Wage and Hour compliance.

54. Question: What is the reason for placing some traditional sick time in employees' PTO accounts at the start of PTO?

Answer: This is a "cushion" of time that is being allowed only once, when the PTO program starts. It acknowledges that some workers may be ill at the commencement of PTO, well before they have had a chance to build up the "sick component" of their PTO accounts. It also helps to show employees that PTO is fair and reasonable.

55. **Question:** Why do companies that are unionized seem to implement PTO for nonbargaining unit workers first ?

Answer: It is usually easier to implement PTO first with nonbargaining unit employees. PTO is a bargaining item under terms of the union's contract. However, companies then use PTO design for nonbargaining units when renegotiating contracts.

56. **Question:** Is there any research on the effectiveness of PTO plans? How do they compare with traditional leave packages (like separate annual vacation and sick time, etc.)?

Answer: I suggest that you see the CCH *Annual Absence Study* and the U.S. Chamber of Commerce's *Annual Study on Employee Benefits*. Both studies research the effectiveness of PTO and other absentee control programs and annually report their findings.

57. **Question:** Does an employee have to use another five days of PTO before accessing CAT if the employee returns to work after being out on CAT and then has a relapse?

Answer: Companies often waive the five-day requirement if a relapse occurs within a specified time period (e.g., one week) after returning to work.

58. **Question:** How do most high-tech employers handle sick time and personal time off for administrative/technical nonexempt employees (e.g., administrative assistants, administrative/technical nonexempt employees) who work in the "office" versus those on the "production" floor?

Answer: Traditionally "office" staff had different amounts of sick and vacation time than "production" workers. Today, differences between the two groups are disappearing.